"*Operating in the Power of God's* resource reflecting the richness of ... avail-able for every believer. As you read th... elieve you will be inspired to engage life from the lens of God's grace. With an abundance of biblical insight and personal experiences, my good friend Robert Henderson has connected together many aspects of grace into a wholesome perspective for this modern era. This comprehensive resource needs to be in the collection of every believer. It will equip and impart you with knowledge, wisdom and insight into the heart of God that you can hold with you in every season of your life."

Ché Ahn, senior pastor, HRock Church;
president, Harvest International Ministry;
international chancellor, Wagner University

"Key scriptures and themes are emphasized and highlighted by the Holy Spirit over the decades. These truths are in the Word of God, but by the Spirit of Revelation, they suddenly seem to pop off the page in strategic moments of time. Not only do these truths become restored to the Body of Christ, but the Lord also raises up a 'voice that can be heard.' This is the case with the message concerning the grace of God and the messenger of Robert Henderson. Both the truth and the herald of that truth have found favor before God and man. Robert Henderson's latest addition to his gallant works is valuable and needed. I applaud the focus, clarity and character that this dear man brings to the Body of Christ in this hour. Well done. In fact, I hear the Spirit of the Lord saying, 'Very well done!'"

James W. Goll, founder, God Encounters Ministries;
author, communications trainer, consultant
and recording artist

OPERATING IN THE
POWER
OF
GOD'S
GRACE

OPERATING IN THE
POWER
OF
GOD'S
GRACE

DISCOVER THE SECRET OF FRUITFULNESS

ROBERT
HENDERSON

Chosen

a division of Baker Publishing Group
Minneapolis, Minnesota

Published by Chosen Books
11400 Hampshire Avenue South
Bloomington, Minnesota 55438
www.chosenbooks.com

Chosen Books is a division of
Baker Publishing Group, Grand Rapids, Michigan

Printed in the United States of America

Library of Congress Cataloging-in-Publication Data
Names: Henderson, Robert, author.
Title: Operating in the power of God's grace : discover the secret of fruitfulness / Robert Henderson.
Description: Bloomington, Minnesota : Chosen Books, [2019]
Identifiers: LCCN 2019021621 | ISBN 9780800799489 (trade paperback) | ISBN 9781493420483 (ebook)
Subjects: LCSH: Grace (Theology) | Christian life.
Classification: LCC BT761.3 .H56 2019 | DDC 234—dc23
LC record available at https://lccn.loc.gov/2019021621

Scripture quotations are from the New King James Version®. Copyright © 1982 by Thomas Nelson. Used by permission. All rights reserved.

Cover design by Rob Williams, InsideOutCreativeArts

19 20 21 22 23 24 25   7 6 5 4 3 2 1

Without Mary, my wife of over forty years, I would have less of a view and understanding of the grace of God. She is my encourager, my counselor and one who brings necessary prophetic insight into my life at significant and pivotal times. In short, she is an expression of God's grace toward me. I dedicate this book to her. I am so grateful for her undying faithfulness, loyalty and love to me and to our family. Thanks, sweetie, for being God's grace personified.

Contents

Foreword by Mark Chironna   11

1. Freed to Be Fruitful   13

2. The Look of God   45

3. Seeking Mercy, Finding Grace   59

4. Grace versus Works   73

5. The Grease of God   89

6. Grace Attached to Purpose   105

7. Gifts and Grace   123

8. The Supernatural Ability of Grace   141

9. The Gift of People   159

10. Limitless Living   171

11. Moving in Grace   187

12. The Finishing Touch of Grace   199

Foreword

Perhaps the most significant existential crisis of our times is tied to the question of "Who am I?" Identity crisis has always been an issue, yet in the consumer-driven post-Christian culture in which we find ourselves, we are attempting to know ourselves as individuals who are self-conscious rather than as persons made in the image and likeness of God.

When God created Adam, He declared, "It is not good for man to be alone." Famed twentieth-century English anthropologist Gregory Bateson said, "It takes two to know one." In essence, Bateson was echoing God's evaluation that it isn't good for any of us to be individuals. We cannot know ourselves by ourselves. The moment we attempt to define ourselves independent of the triune God, we deny ourselves the grace of knowing who we truly are. And when we fail to know who we truly are based on who God made us to be, we fail to avail ourselves of the grace of God by the Holy Spirit to become all He intends us to be.

11

The Holy Spirit influences us from the depths to bring us to full awareness of who we are, where we are going and how we will arrive there. That influence of the Spirit involves His uncreated energy, which is constantly moving toward us and in us to empower us to fulfill all His intent. What the Scriptures call that activity of the Spirit is "grace"—a topic often overlooked and often misinterpreted. Grace is immensely powerful and essential to the perfecting experiences and totality of our expression in life, which flows out of an awareness of our God-given uniqueness as persons. Learning to lean on the indwelling Spirit to be all we are called to be and to become all we are called to become is the fruit of this amazing grace.

Robert Henderson is a great communicator, and he has some compelling insights on the grace of God. He makes that grace accessible to us at the practical place in life of how to put one foot in front of another by the Spirit, and then to take the next easiest step of faith by grace into our God-intended future. *Operating in the Power of God's Grace* is worth the read and, more than that, worth heeding and applying. Enjoy the read, and make the most of it by acting on what you have read.

Dr. Mark Chironna, Church On The Living Edge,
Mark Chironna Ministries, Longwood, Florida

ONE

Freed to Be Fruitful

There is a cry in every believer to be fruitful. It is inbred in us. We want our lives to matter and to count. We want to feel as though we are accomplishing something worthwhile. I know there will be the detractors who say that our identity is not based in what we do, but in who we are. They will point out that we must not live life from a performance perspective, feeling good about ourselves based on how well we perform, rather than on who God says we are. I would absolutely agree with this. From having the right idea about who we are, however, we are to produce an impact and make a difference with our lives. We are to be fulfilling our God-ordained reason for being alive on the planet. The Bible actually teaches that each one of us has a divine reason for being here. The apostle Paul tells us in Ephesians 2:10 that things were planned beforehand for us: "For we are His workmanship, created in Christ Jesus for good works, which God prepared beforehand that we should walk in them."

We were created for good works. This is why we crave being effective. It is built into us. It is part of the divine nature we have received from God. Doing good works does not just imply living morally sound lives. Good works are about fulfilling those things that God prepared *beforehand*, which we are to walk in. This all flows out of our being His *workmanship*, which is the Greek word *poiema*. It means "a product," or a "thing that is made."* From *poiema* we get our word *poem*, so it is a creative work. When we look at art, read poetry or enjoy some kind of artistic piece, what we are looking at actually reveals the artist who created it. The nature of the artist is hidden within the artistic display. So it is within us. As those who belong to Jesus and are born again, the nature of the Artist is revealed in us and through us. Who He is, is seen from our lives. This is seen in the *good works* flowing out of us as His *workmanship*.

I think it is interesting that this verse in Ephesians speaks of us having been *created* in Christ Jesus for these good works. *Created* is in the past tense. This means that before we existed, this was already done. What we are here to accomplish was preordained for us. We did not enter the earth without reason or purpose. The day we were born, we entered the earth with a divine and heavenly agenda. There were already plans of God that we were to fulfill. This requires fruitfulness.

Standing above the Crowd

In some circles, having a desire for success and accomplishment is looked down on. For instance, in the Australian cul-

---

*Note that the definitions I provide of Greek and Hebrew words throughout are all taken from *Strong's Concordance*, Orion Systems Version 3.0.3 (2010–2017), https://itunes.apple.com/dm/app/strongs-concordance/id405005619?mt=8.

ture (which I love, by the way), there is something referred to as the "tall poppy syndrome." Poppies are beautiful flowers, yet this phrase is used in a degrading way to describe anyone who wants to stand out above others. It is okay if you are beautiful and blend in with others. If, however, you try to stand above the crowd in any kind of way, you are accused of having this tall poppy syndrome. This accusation is used to make everyone blend in so that no one person is above any other. As my Australian friends tell me, this is healthy in one sense, in that it creates humility. In another sense, however, it destroys creativity and uniqueness and thwarts people's desire to have a big impact. If they try to stand out and be significant, they are put back in their place.

This kind of syndrome is not just relegated to the Australian culture. It also appears in other cultures, families and settings. In some religious circles, the desire to rise and shine is ridiculed and looked down on. David found himself fighting against this attitude, when all he was trying to do was be faithful to what was inside him. First Samuel 17:26–29 tells us the story of David's brothers ridiculing him because he dared to stand up:

> Then David spoke to the men who stood by him, saying, "What shall be done for the man who kills this Philistine and takes away the reproach from Israel? For who is this uncircumcised Philistine, that he should defy the armies of the living God?"
>
> And the people answered him in this manner, saying, "So shall it be done for the man who kills him."
>
> Now Eliab his oldest brother heard when he spoke to the men; and Eliab's anger was aroused against David, and he said, "Why did you come down here? And with whom have you left those few sheep in the wilderness? I know your pride

and the insolence of your heart, for you have come down to see the battle."

And David said, "What have I done now? Is there not a cause?"

A giant needs to be defeated, and everyone else is cowering before him. David comes on the scene, and what is inside him will not allow him to tolerate what others are tolerating. He wants to know what will be granted to the one who kills this giant and delivers Israel. When Eliab hears David's question, he is appalled. He accuses David of the tall poppy syndrome.

Eliab does not know who David really is. All he sees him as is his little brother. David, however, will not allow Eliab to subdue what is in him through his accusations. He stands up against them and first responds, "What have I done now?" In other words, "I am tired of you pressing me down. I am weary of allowing you to try to fashion me, and weary of your prejudice against me, trying to steal away my destiny and what I know is in me."

David then utters the famous words, "Is there not a cause?" The word *cause* in the Hebrew is *dabar*. It can mean several different things, one of the ideas being, "Is there not a word?" David could have been saying, "Don't we have a word from God on this matter? Why are you just sitting around in fear, doing nothing? Let's rise up and move at the word of the Lord." David was jealous for the word of the Lord over the Israelites as a nation. This giant was challenging it. The word used is that Goliath was *defying* the armies of Israel. *Defy* in the Hebrew means "to pull off by stripping." Goliath, through his words, was stripping Israel of its faith and identity, and was bringing shame. David came on the scene and stood up to resist this.

Many times, there are forces in the unseen realm that attack our identity. They question who we really are and the destiny that is assigned to us. We must have the spirit of David, which will arise and challenge these voices. We must not cower before them, as the armies of Israel did. We must stand up out of the tall poppy syndrome and bring a victory for ourselves and even for others. We must contend for the word of God that is declaring the future He has for us. This is what David was doing, and what we must do as well. Each of us must have the sense of a prophetic destiny that comes from God. We must have some sense of an awareness of who we are as His workmanship. Then we must let that fashion us, and not the ideas of others or even the culture we are part of. This is somewhat like what Paul spoke of in Romans 12:1–2:

> I beseech you therefore, brethren, by the mercies of God, that you present your bodies a living sacrifice, holy, acceptable to God, which is your reasonable service. And do not be conformed to this world, but be transformed by the renewing of your mind, that you may prove what is that good and acceptable and perfect will of God.

We are not to allow this world and its system to form us. We must allow what God is saying about us as His workmanship to be that deciding factor. Through the renewing of our mind with the principles of God's Word, presence and ideas, we are shaped into the image of the One who created us. We begin to think of ourselves as He thinks of us. We do not think arrogantly or haughtily of ourselves, but neither do we think less of ourselves. We think according to the measure of faith that has been granted to us. Romans 12:3 tells us to think soberly, according to the measure of faith that has been given to us:

> For I say, through the grace given to me, to everyone who is among you, not to think of himself more highly than he ought to think, but to think soberly, as God has dealt to each one a measure of faith.

Faith is something that helps determine the way we see ourselves. Sometimes we think faith is only about the way we see God. Faith, however, is also about how we see who we are when we are connected to God. According to the measure of faith given to us, we are able to see who we are in God. In other words, we believe what God says about us. We do not let the opinions of others shape us. We must gain our identity expressly from the Lord and His Word.

Jesus Himself had to do this. When He came to Nazareth, the people's view of Him was determined by who His family was. If Jesus had allowed it, the opinion of the people would have reduced Him down to who they perceived His family to be. Yet Jesus had an awareness of who He was from His heavenly Father. Mark 6:2–3 shows people becoming offended at Him because they wanted to diminish who He was:

> And when the Sabbath had come, He began to teach in the synagogue. And many hearing Him were astonished, saying, "Where did this Man get these things? And what wisdom is this which is given to Him, that such mighty works are performed by His hands! Is this not the carpenter, the Son of Mary, and brother of James, Joses, Judas, and Simon? And are not His sisters here with us?" So they were offended at Him.

When people stand up and begin to refuse the labels, tags and brands others seek to place on them, those others will become offended. Those others want everyone simply to be part of the crowd, and they rarely change or have an impact on anything. In fact, they really do not want to see change, and anyone who seeks to bring change can become their enemy. They are content with the status quo.

The problem is that God has put into the hearts of many "tall poppies" a spirit that cannot be content with this. They have a different spirit, as Caleb had. Caleb and Joshua were two of the twelve spies Moses sent to spy out the land. Ten came back with a bad report, while these two came back with a report full of faith and hope. Numbers 14:24 shows God confirming and blessing Caleb in particular because of the spirit and attitude within him: "But My servant Caleb, because he has a different spirit in him and has followed Me fully, I will bring into the land where he went, and his descendants shall inherit it."

God promises to bring Caleb into the land of promise because he has a *different* spirit. Is there a *different* spirit in us today? Do we have something in us that sets us apart from the rest of the culture, which is satisfied just to be also-rans? Are we a people who desire to believe God for great things? Scripture says God loves to be identified with people who have these desires and this spirit:

> And truly if they had called to mind that country from which they had come out, they would have had opportunity to return. But now they desire a better, that is, a heavenly country. Therefore God is not ashamed to be called their God, for He has prepared a city for them.
>
> Hebrews 11:15–16

God loves to be called these people's God. He loves people who will not be satisfied and will not seek opportunity to return to the comfortable. This different spirit within them stirs His heart toward them. I want to be this kind of person. I do not want to settle. I want to press in and push into the fullness of what I was made for. As someone once said, "Why would you seek to fit in when you were made to stand out?"

Labeled and Marked by Grace

I would call your attention to one more Scripture that identifies the kind of spirit the world has, which seeks to make us conform. First John 3:1–3 shows us that the world does not know who we are:

> Behold what manner of love the Father has bestowed on us, that we should be called children of God! Therefore the world does not know us, because it did not know Him. Beloved, now we are children of God; and it has not yet been revealed what we shall be, but we know that when He is revealed, we shall be like Him, for we shall see Him as He is. And everyone who has this hope in Him purifies himself, just as He is pure.

The apostle John clearly said *the world does not know us*. If the world does not know who we are, then why do we continually allow it to tell us who we are? Through the world's influence, others consistently seek to brand us, label us and mark us with who they want us to be. We must consistently push back against this.

Even the three Hebrew children who stood for their God in Babylon had to make sure they did *not* allow that system to tell them who they were (see Daniel 1:6–7). Their Hebrew names were Hananiah, Mishael and Azariah, yet we know them by their Babylonian names of Shadrach, Meshach and

Abed-Nego. These were the names given to them in the land of their captivity. Why was this done? Their captors were seeking to fashion these young men's identities and cause them to think of themselves differently. That world system was seeking to tell them who they were.

The young men's three Hebrew names spoke of who God was in their lives. *Hananiah* in the Hebrew means "God has favored." *Mishael* means "Who is like God?" *Azariah* means "God has helped." By changing the names, their captors were seeking to erase from them an awareness of the God they served and therefore their God-ordained identity. These three, however, would not allow it. They stood and refused the label and tags they were given. They might not have been able to maintain their original names in their circumstances, but they did not have to allow the name changes to form their thinking.

Neither do we today. Despite all its efforts, the demonically inspired world system has no right to determine who we see ourselves to be. According to Scripture, we are the children of God. We carry His nature, character and identity. His love fashions us. The world does not have any concept of who we are. In fact, we ourselves do not even fully see who we are, but marked by grace, we are confident that we will be like Him before all is said and done. This hope and desire in us pushes us to purify ourselves constantly, as He is pure. We are breaking out of the image the world would make us into, and we are progressively moving into the image of the One who loves us deeply.

All of this is absolutely essential to bearing fruit. We cannot produce what we do not understand ourselves to be producers of. This is where grace comes in. The apostle Paul said he was what he was by the grace of God. First Corinthians

15:10 shows him boasting in the grace of God: "But by the grace of God I am what I am, and His grace toward me was not in vain; but I labored more abundantly than they all, yet not I, but the grace of God which was with me."

Notice that Paul attributes to grace what he has become. He also declares, however, that from this grace he labored more abundantly than anyone else. This means that grace to Paul was not a license to stop putting forth effort. In fact, grace was an empowerment for him to work more tirelessly than others. Grace does not give us license to be lazy or unmotivated. Grace will inspire us from within to give our lives to obtain all God has called us to be. Grace will push us forward and will not allow us to rest until we become all that is in the heart of God for us. We will get into this more, but suffice it to say here that we do not produce out of our own efforts. It is grace in us that drives us forth to become fruitful, and grace that produces the passion of God in us and through us.

Running the Race Set before Us

As I said in the beginning, we all desire to be fruitful. We want our lives to count. I am a big fan of the holiday classic movie *It's a Wonderful Life*. George Bailey, played by Jimmy Stewart, finds himself in a devastating place where he becomes convinced that it would have been better for everyone, including himself, if he had never been born. He feels as if his life has been for no good reason. He has lived a frustrated and unfulfilled life because he thinks it should have gone another way. It takes heavenly intervention for him to come to the realization that he has a blessed life.

His life has, in fact, had an impact on countless others because he was alive. Without his life, others would have had completely different and worse lives. This can be true for us as well. When we surrender our lives to the Lordship of Jesus, He is the Author and Finisher of our faith. We must allow Him the right and privilege to take our lives into the path He has desired. Hebrews 12:1–2 gives us insight into this idea:

> Therefore we also, since we are surrounded by so great a cloud of witnesses, let us lay aside every weight, and the sin which so easily ensnares us, and let us run with endurance the race that is set before us, looking unto Jesus, the author and finisher of our faith, who for the joy that was set before Him endured the cross, despising the shame, and has sat down at the right hand of the throne of God.

I want to point out that we have a *race that is set before us*. This means we may not have chosen the exact path we are on. There was a race chosen for us. In other words, there are things about the path we have been on that we might go back and change if we could, yet God wants and needs us on this course, just like George Bailey. We are to keep our eyes on Jesus and trust Him. We are to run with endurance this race set before us. This endurance comes from the grace of God in our lives. It is not self-produced. It is supernatural in nature.

I have always liked to run. I was never a fast sprinter in short races. I was not even the fastest in long races. What I could do, however, was run for a long time and run a long way. I have endurance. The way I run and keep on running when I want to stop is to set goals. I remember my high school coaches taking us out on deserted roads and having us run back to the school. Many of the guys would catch rides in passing cars coming back toward the school. Before they would get close enough for the coaches to see them, they would get out of the cars and pretend to be out of breath from their "long run."

I would not do this. I would run all the way back in. My personal goal was to make sure I did not walk any of the course, but to run the whole way. I always have enjoyed challenging myself. My competition has not been against others, but rather to best myself, when I can. As I would run, my body, muscles and lungs would be screaming for me to stop and walk. I would not allow it. Telephone poles lined the roadway, and I would look down the road and set the next telephone pole as my goal. I would tell myself, *You are going to run to this next telephone pole. You are going to keep this pace and not stop.* As I would reach that pole, I would then set the next pole as my new goal. By doing this, I would run all the way back to school without stopping.

I learned to set goals and not stop until I reached them. This was, and is, the key to my endurance. I discovered a grace that produced endurance in my life. When I did not think I could make it to that next pole, as I tried, a grace would come that empowered me. I discovered that I had more endurance than I thought because of a grace in my life. I found that what I thought I could not do, I actually could do when I tried. There was a grace that would manifest in my life that strengthened me to do what I naturally thought impossible.

Jesus experienced this as well. In Luke 22:41–44, we see Him battling and struggling in the Garden of Gethsemane with His own will and desires:

And He was withdrawn from them about a stone's throw, and He knelt down and prayed, saying, "Father, if it is Your will, take this cup away from Me; nevertheless not My will, but Yours, be done." Then an angel appeared to Him from heaven, strengthening Him. And being in agony, He prayed more earnestly. Then His sweat became like great drops of blood falling down to the ground.

As Jesus struggled to surrender to the will of the Father, He set His heart to obey. As this surrender came, an angel came with grace from heaven that empowered Him to pray even more earnestly and effectively, past human ability. His sweat dropping with blood speaks of the deep distress and stress Jesus felt. Even He was unable to face all of this in His own human strength. His power to accomplish the will of God came from a heavenly dimension as He sought to satisfy the passion of His Father. With endurance He ran His race, but only through heavenly empowerment and grace. We, too, must have this influence in our lives. Only then will we be able to produce the fruit we are called to produce and finish the course we have been given to run.

Overcoming with Grace

As we finish this chapter, I want to talk about five things that grace helps us overcome, that we might be fruitful. My ultimate purpose in this book is not to discuss theological ideas, as important as that might be. The reason for this book is to release an empowerment through God's grace to make us effective and fruitful. Here are five things that can prevent fruitfulness but grace can help us overcome: not being planted, not embracing the pruning process, a spirit of barrenness, stagnation in our spiritual walk and a Jezebel spirit. Let's look at them one at a time, to better understand what they are and why we must overcome them. As you and I overcome by grace these five reasons for unfruitfulness, fruit will become the norm for our lives.

Overcoming not being planted

One thing a lack of fruit can be traced back to is *not being planted*. Psalm 1:1–3 tells us that those who bear fruit are planted:

> Blessed is the man who walks not in the counsel of the ungodly, nor stands in the path of sinners, nor sits in the seat of the scornful; but his delight is in the law of the LORD, and in His law he meditates day and night. He shall be like a tree planted by the rivers of water, that brings forth its fruit in its season, whose leaf also shall not wither; and whatever he does shall prosper.

Notice that a man's *planting* is in the law/Word of the Lord. If our lives are based on and in the Word of God and that Word is what rules our life, we will bear fruit. It is amazing how many people feel as though they can make up their own rules and follow their own agenda and still get the kind of life they want. It does not work that way. My wife, Mary, grew up in a military family. Her father was a career United States Air Force enlisted man. As a result of this, they lived on many military bases across the world during Mary's growing-up years. She tells the story of the enlisted men who would come to their house, looking for help and companionship in their hard times. Their lives would be in shambles because of the choices they had made. Even as one who did not yet know the Lord, Mary looked at these people's choices and decided she did not want the life those choices had produced.

If a young girl can figure this out, surely people who have been in the atmosphere of the Church can. Yet I watch as people who have grown up in the Church cohabitate with others outside marriage, indulge excessively in alcohol and abusive substances, use language a sailor would not use and make choices completely contrary to the Bible. They then are astonished when things begin to fall to pieces in their lives. Many times, they want someone to pray a prayer in a moment to fix what years of wrong choices have created. This is impossible. The only way to fix the problem is to repent and line our lives up with the Word of God. If we get our lives planted in His Word, we will bear fruit in our season, our leaf will not wither and whatever we do will prosper. This is the key to breaking unfruitfulness and having the life of impact we desire.

Overcoming not embracing the pruning process

A second thing that can cause unfruitfulness is *not embracing the pruning process*. Jesus said in John 15:1–2 that God is after maximum fruit. Even when we bear fruit, He prunes us that we might produce more: "I am the true vine, and My Father is the vinedresser. Every branch in Me that does not bear fruit He takes away; and every branch that bears fruit He prunes, that it may bear more fruit."

We would think that if we are bearing fruit, this would be sufficient. This passage clearly tells us, however, that when we bear fruit, God desires more. This gives us some insight into the mind and thought process of the Lord. He presses us to our ultimate and absolute potential. He does not want anything left on the table, so to speak. He wants every potential He placed in us realized. He brings this to reality by pruning that which is already bearing and producing fruit.

Pruning is a process whereby what is taking life, yet producing nothing worthwhile, is cut off. In other words, if a vine has a life flow moving in it, but it is not producing to its maximum capacity, a wise vinedresser will prune that vine. One of the purposes of pruning a grapevine is to reduce "shading." In other words, the leaves can become so many that the vine and shoots become covered and the sun cannot reach what is necessary. This causes smaller and less desirable grapes. Pruning cuts away the right amount of shoot growth so the vine can produce the best grapes.

God does the same thing with us. Anything that *shades* us and does not allow the influence of His grace to touch us must be removed. One thing that shades us is a reliance on our own strength and ability. Through God's pruning process, He removes the confidence we would have in our own strength and causes us to rely on Him. Paul spoke of this in several places. Philippians 3:3–9 gives us insight into how Paul lost and laid aside all confidence in his own righteousness and power, putting his entire trust in Jesus and who He is:

> For we are the circumcision, who worship God in the Spirit, rejoice in Christ Jesus, and have no confidence in the flesh, though I also might have confidence in the flesh. If anyone else thinks he may have confidence in the flesh, I more so: circumcised the eighth day, of the stock of Israel, of the tribe of Benjamin, a Hebrew of the Hebrews; concerning the law, a Pharisee; concerning zeal, persecuting the church; concerning the righteousness which is in the law, blameless.

But what things were gain to me, these I have counted loss for Christ. Yet indeed I also count all things loss for the excellence of the knowledge of Christ Jesus my Lord, for whom I have suffered the loss of all things, and count them as rubbish, that I may gain Christ and be found in Him, not having my own righteousness, which is from the law, but that which is through faith in Christ, the righteousness which is from God by faith.

Paul said if anybody ought to be able to have confidence in himself, it was he. Yet he realized that even in his greatest place of strength, it would never be enough. He had to lay it aside and put his entire confidence in Jesus and what He had done for him. Paul actually said he counted it loss. He said he was willing to lose everything for the treasure of knowing Christ Jesus his Lord.

Losing confidence in our own abilities and strength can be a hard process to go through, yet it is necessary. Only in our weakness is the Lord's strength made perfect. In 2 Corinthians 12:9, Paul alludes to the secret of living from weakness that releases new realms of grace: "And He said to me, 'My grace is sufficient for you, for My strength is made perfect in weakness.' Therefore most gladly I will rather boast in my infirmities, that the power of Christ may rest upon me."

Jesus revealed to Paul this powerful principle that His strength is manifested powerfully in our weakest state. To get us to this state of "weakness" where we have no confidence in our own strength requires the pruning of the Lord. The shade we have had our confidence in has to be removed so that our only hope is in Jesus and His grace. We are then ready to be trusted with fruitfulness. The Lord actually did this with Gideon, instructing him to send home from among the troops any men who were fearful before a battle. Doing this would remove those who would contaminate others with their fear. This is because fear is contagious. If you make room for it, it will completely consume you and even others around you. The other reason, however, was that the Lord did not want His people mistakenly believing they had won the victory because of their superior numbers. Judges 7:2–3 tells us,

> And the LORD said to Gideon, "The people who are with you are too many for Me to give the Midianites into their hands, lest Israel claim glory for itself against Me, saying, 'My own hand has saved me.' Now therefore, proclaim in the hearing of the people, saying, 'Whoever is fearful and afraid, let him turn and depart at once from Mount Gilead.'" And twenty-two thousand of the people returned, and ten thousand remained.

Before it was over, God had reduced the army down to three hundred. From these three hundred He defeated a much superior army. Everyone knew it was the Lord who had done it. God had to prune and strip Gideon and the army so that in their weakness, He could manifest His strength.

The Lord does the same thing with us. In a dream I had several years ago, the Lord appeared to me. In the beginning of the dream I was standing outside a cave. I could sense the Lord in the Spirit, but I did not *see* Him in the natural. I knew, however, that He had gone into the cave. I was very hungry for His presence and anointing, so I pursued Him into the cave. When I was just barely inside, Jesus' face then appeared and two mantles were released. They floated to me, and I knew they were the mantles of the Spirit and of power. Paul spoke of them in 1 Corinthians 2:2–5:

For I determined not to know anything among you except Jesus Christ and Him crucified. I was with you in weakness, in fear, and in much trembling. And my speech and my preaching were not with persuasive words of human wisdom, but in demonstration of the Spirit and of power, that your faith should not be in the wisdom of men but in the power of God.

Notice that Paul was with the people in weakness, fear and trembling. In this state the power, glory and grace of God were made manifest and Paul demonstrated the Spirit and power. These were the mantles I received in my dream as I pursued Jesus and His face appeared to me. In my dream, Jesus then continued deeper into the cave. Even though I now had what I was originally pursuing Him for, I continued following after Him. As we got deeper into the cave, suddenly Jesus appeared in His full bodily capacity. I saw Him in His fullness. As I reached Him in my pursuit, I reached out and touched Him on His shoulder. When I made contact, He stopped, turned and looked over His shoulder at me. I then spoke to Him. I did not know what was going to come out of my mouth. What I heard myself say in this moment was, *What must I do to love You more?*

Looking at me, Jesus responded with one word: *Separation!*

The dream ended, and I woke up wondering what it had meant. I had an idea, but it would take me several years to fully understand. You must know that my wife and I had been blessed with a very fruitful ministry. We had raised and led the largest charismatic church in our city. I was on TV five days a week. We had a functioning Bible school that was training ministers and others. I had a large staff and in many ways had great influence in our city and region. When the Lord said *Separation!* I felt He was asking me to lay all of that aside. He was pressing me to "separate" myself from all He had blessed me with and what was now my strength.

This is exactly what Mary and I did in the months following this encounter. I did not realize it then, but God was taking me through a Gideon place of pruning to reduce me down, that He might exalt me in due time. We did, in fact, walk through this place for several years. I believe God was proving me and seeing if I would allow Him to bring me into weakness, that His strength might be made manifest in me.

During this season, we transitioned from pastoring this very powerful church to having a traveling ministry. Even though I did not know it at the time, it was like starting over. Contacts had to be made, and networking had to occur so other people would get to know me. Establishing myself as one who could minister to the Body of Christ at large was essential. This took years to happen. I discovered that the kind of word I had spoken as a pastor to a local church was not sufficient for speaking to the Church at large. I had to dig deeper and develop a more apostolic and prophetic ministry that supplied to churches what the local ministry was unable to give. Otherwise, there would have been no need for my ministry.

Plus, we left a church where we were greatly loved and honored, and we stepped into a realm where we were unknown and even sometimes were suspect. Whereas we had previously enjoyed a strong network of relationships, we were now thrust into a place of isolation. We were *separated*, just as the Lord had spoken to me. In the midst of all this, God was dealing with us, pruning us and causing us to learn of Him in a new and significant way. At times this was painful, scary and awkward, and it caused much questioning in us. In the midst of it all, however, we sought to keep our eyes on Jesus, the Author and Finisher of our faith (see Hebrews 12:2). He was faithful to navigate us through this time, into our present state and function in life and ministry.

I believe this is what God does to His choicest vessels. This is what He did to the apostle Paul—not that I consider myself a Paul. I just know, as many people do, the pain and struggle of having a calling on our lives and the place of fear and uncertainty it can propel us into. Yet what abides in us is a sense and awareness that God is preparing us for His use, to have an impact on the world. When God sent Ananias to Saul of Tarsus with a word in Acts 9:15–16, He told Ananias that Saul was a chosen vessel: "But the Lord said to him, 'Go, for he is a chosen vessel of Mine to bear My name before Gentiles, kings, and the children of Israel. For I will show him how many things he must suffer for My name's sake.'" The Lord declared that Saul was His chosen vessel. As a result, Saul would be required to suffer. The suffering would not give the Lord some morbid enjoyment, but rather would reduce Paul down so that every confidence in the flesh would be removed. His only confidence would be in the power and grace of who Jesus is. Anyone the Lord uses significantly will be brought to a place of knowing it is all of grace. I must have everything I am living under—every shade—removed so that the only thing I am under and have confidence in is the Lord Himself. At this point, I am ready to bear fruit.

As Jesus spoke of the whole fruit-bearing process and the pruning God does, He made a statement we must come to realize is true. In John 15:5, He declared that we are incapable of producing what God desires without our strength coming from Him: "I am the vine, you are the branches. He who abides in Me, and I in him, bears much fruit; for without Me you can do nothing." Jesus is letting it be known that only from a real union and connection with Him and His life will we bear fruit. The awareness that it is only by His grace is imperative to our bearing fruit and the Father being glorified.

Overcoming a spirit of barrenness

A third issue that can cause unfruitfulness is *a spirit of barrenness*. In 1 Samuel 1:10–11, Hannah is crying out for a son. She is tormented by her inability to conceive and bring forth a child. She is unfruitful:

> And she was in bitterness of soul, and prayed to the LORD and wept in anguish.
> Then she made a vow and said, "O LORD of hosts, if You will indeed look on the affliction of Your maidservant and remember me, and not forget Your maidservant, but will give Your maidservant a male child, then I will give him to the LORD all the days of his life, and no razor shall come upon his head."

Out of her bitterness and pain, Hannah makes a vow to God. She promises that if He will give her a male child, she will give that child to the Lord and His purposes all his life. Eli, the high priest in those days, sees her as she prays and thinks she is drunk. Verses 14–18 chronicle the next part of this story. As she prays and her lips move without sound, Eli rebukes her, thinking she is a wicked woman:

> So Eli said to her, "How long will you be drunk? Put your wine away from you!"

But Hannah answered and said, "No, my lord, I am a woman of sorrowful spirit. I have drunk neither wine nor intoxicating drink, but have poured out my soul before the LORD. Do not consider your maidservant a wicked woman, for out of the abundance of my complaint and grief I have spoken until now."

Then Eli answered and said, "Go in peace, and the God of Israel grant your petition which you have asked of Him."

And she said, "Let your maidservant find favor in your sight." So the woman went her way and ate, and her face was no longer sad.

Recognizing his mistake, Eli declares a blessing over Hannah and her request. Notice what happens. She gets up, goes her way, eats and is no longer sad. The moment Eli as high priest blesses her and declares her request granted, this whole spirit of barrenness comes off her. This is why she is sad no longer. What had been controlling her is now broken. The result of this time is that she and her husband are intimate and she conceives because the spirit of barrenness has now been lifted from her.

To see fruitfulness come through our lives, we must deal at times with this spirit of barrenness. The devil will seek to use it to keep us from bearing fruit and advancing the Kingdom of God. As Hannah's request was granted, her desire for a child was met. God also had His need met.

Allow me to take a moment to explain what I mean by God having a need. We would agree that God is the all-sufficient One who has no needs. Yet God has a plan and purpose He desires to see fulfilled in the earth. In Revelation 10:7, this plan, this work of redeeming all things back to Himself, is called *the mystery of God*: "But in the days of the sounding of the seventh angel, when he is about to sound, the mystery of God would be finished, as He declared to His servants the prophets." The complete work of redemption, the completion of this *mystery of God*, requires much activity on the part of God's people as He reclaims the nations to Himself. Part of this redemption process is having ministry gifts in operation that influence the Church, which in turn influences the culture.

In Samuel's day, God needed the prophet Samuel to be His voice in the nation of Israel. Otherwise, what God desired to occur in that time might have been postponed. So when I speak of God having a need, I am speaking of Him having whatever is needed to see His purpose done in the earth and see the *mystery of God* being brought to absolute fulfillment. God needed a prophet/priest in Hannah's time to reclaim the nation from the corrupted priesthood of Eli and his sons. This corrupted priesthood that Samuel grew up serving had not allowed the passion of God to be carried out. God's need was for a prophet in that time to shape the course of nations.

There are times God will allow us to walk through places of bitterness and barrenness to bring us to a place where we are willing to surrender all. This is what happened to Hannah. God allowed her to walk through such a place of barrenness that it formed in her a willingness to do the unthinkable— give up her firstborn son. When she came to this place, God then had His need met in Samuel, a prophet/priest who would manifest God's heart and turn a nation to Him.

When Hannah was willing to put the need of God above her own desires, her barrenness was broken. This is what Jesus said in Matthew 6:33: "But seek first the kingdom of God and His righteousness, and all these things shall be added to you." When we place the *need* of God ahead of our own desires and seek His Kingdom first, *all* other things are added to us. This is a reference to our needs being met and fulfilled. It is interesting that when we place God's need ahead of ours, our own cries are answered. This is exactly what happened to Hannah. Her barrenness was eradicated, and fruitfulness came. She even had three more sons and two daughters. First Samuel 2:21 shows the fruitfulness that was unlocked in and through Hannah because of her sacrifice: "And the LORD visited Hannah, so that she conceived and bore three sons and two daughters. Meanwhile the child Samuel grew before the Lord." God had His prophet, who was growing up before Him, while Hannah received the family she so desperately craved. Her fruitlessness was replaced with abounding fruitfulness.

Overcoming stagnation in our spiritual walk

A fourth thing to deal with that can cause unfruitfulness is *stagnation in our spiritual walk*. Peter cautions about this in 2 Peter 1:5–8 and speaks of *adding* to our faith on a consistent basis:

> But also for this very reason, giving all diligence, add to your faith virtue, to virtue knowledge, to knowledge self-control, to self-control perseverance, to perseverance godliness, to godliness brotherly kindness, and to brotherly kindness love. For if these things are yours and abound, you will be neither barren nor unfruitful in the knowledge of our Lord Jesus Christ.

We can begin our walk with the Lord by being fruitful. But if we are not careful and diligent, Peter said, we can become barren and unfruitful.

Jesus spoke of this as well. In Matthew 13, Jesus gives us the parable of the sower and the different soils his seed fell in. Here is how He describes the soil filled with thorns and briars: "Now he who received seed among the thorns is he who hears the word, and the cares of this world and the deceitfulness of riches choke the word, and he becomes unfruitful" (verse 22). Notice that the recipient *becomes unfruitful*. In other words, he was fruitful, but then became unfruitful. This is because there were thorns choking out what was being produced.

This is what Peter was declaring. We must not allow thorns in our hearts and lives to remove our fruitfulness. The best way to make sure of this is to be on the offensive in our faith. We are to diligently *add* some things to our walk with God. We are to be developing virtue, knowledge, self-control, perseverance, godliness, brotherly kindness and love. If we do this, fruitfulness will take care of itself. We will be neither barren nor unfruitful. The thorns will be removed that want to choke out the fruit God desires us to bear.

Overcoming the Jezebel spirit

The fifth and final thing I will mention that can cause unfruitfulness is *the Jezebel spirit*. Jezebel was a wicked woman who ruled Israel with her husband, Ahab. God has nothing good to say about her. She led Israel away from Him and into Baal worship. One of the things she did was castrate men and make them into eunuchs whom she surrounded herself with. She emasculated them, making them unable to reproduce. To be clear, although Jezebel's servants actually were castrated, I am not talking about something a woman would do to a man. I am speaking of this *spirit* and what it does to God's people, both men and women. What happened to those servants in the physical is in essence what can happen to people in the spiritual, and it causes unfruitfulness. Jesus spoke against this spirit in Revelation 2:20–23:

> Nevertheless I have a few things against you, because you allow that woman Jezebel, who calls herself a prophetess, to teach and seduce My servants to commit sexual immorality and eat things sacrificed to idols. And I gave her time to repent of her sexual immorality, and she did not repent. Indeed I will cast her into a sickbed, and those who commit adultery with her into great tribulation, unless they repent of their deeds. I will kill her children with death, and all the churches shall know that I am He who searches the minds and hearts. And I will give to each one of you according to your works.

This spirit, spoken of as *that woman Jezebel* in this Scripture, will create unfruitfulness if its influence is allowed into our lives. To be clear, I believe that what Jesus is speaking of in this passage as a *woman* is a demonic spiritual force. It is the *same* spirit that drove the original Jezebel in the days of Ahab. Notice please that it must not be allowed. Sometimes out of fear of confrontation, or through intimidation, people do not deal with this spirit, and Jezebel flourishes where weakness in people is perceived. Yet if people stand up in authority, Jezebel will not have a place to operate.

There must be boldness when dealing with this spirit. One of its main characteristics is control. Through manipulation, intimidation and domination, this spirit will bring people into submission. It will remove their creativity and allow them to do only what pleases it. We actually see this spirit in operation in 3 John 1:9–10:

> I wrote to the church, but Diotrephes, who loves to have the preeminence among them, does not receive us. Therefore, if

I come, I will call to mind his deeds which he does, prating against us with malicious words. And not content with that, he himself does not receive the brethren, and forbids those who wish to, putting them out of the church.

Diotrephes was a man under the influence of this Jezebel spirit. He loved preeminence. He would not receive apostolic authority. He put anyone out of the church who did not agree with him or submit to him. This is consistent with the Jezebel spirit of control. It subdues anyone who will allow himself or herself to be subdued. The results are many, with one of them being fruitlessness.

Remember, this spirit emasculates people and removes from them the ability to reproduce. This is why, when the Old Testament's Jezebel was finally thrown down and destroyed, the ones willing to do it were those whom she had made eunuchs. Second Kings 9:30–33 shows Jehu on assignment from God to rid Israel of idol worship. He tells Jezebel's eunuchs to throw her down:

> Now when Jehu had come to Jezreel, Jezebel heard of it; and she put paint on her eyes and adorned her head, and looked through a window. Then, as Jehu entered at the gate, she said, "Is it peace, Zimri, murderer of your master?"
>
> And he looked up at the window, and said, "Who is on my side? Who?" So two or three eunuchs looked out at him. Then he said, "Throw her down." So they threw her down, and some of her blood spattered on the wall and on the horses; and he trampled her underfoot.

These eunuchs, who had had their ability to reproduce removed, got their revenge. They were instruments of God's justice against Jezebel and the spirit that drove her. They *threw* her down.

To rid yourself of its influence, you have to throw this spirit down. The Jezebel spirit's desire is to sit in a place of authority and influence. It will manipulate its way into these places. If it has been able to do this, it must be thrown down and removed from the place it occupies. Perhaps you gave it a place in your life through a person. As hard as it might seem, you must put this thing in its place. You have to throw it down, or you will never be free to be you and be fruitful.

Entire structures will lose their God-ordained purpose if Jezebel is allowed to rule and have influence. Once Jezebel is dealt with, however, God will even restore "eunuchs" to a place of fruitfulness. Isaiah 56:3–5 makes such a promise to eunuchs who consider themselves fruitless:

> Do not let the son of the foreigner who has joined himself to the LORD speak, saying, "The LORD has utterly separated me from His people"; nor let the eunuch say, "Here I am, a dry tree." For thus says the LORD: "To the eunuchs who keep My Sabbaths, and choose what pleases Me, and hold fast My covenant, even to them I will give in My house and within My walls a place and a name better than that of sons and daughters; I will give them an everlasting name that shall not be cut off."

When I speak of eunuchs, I am not speaking of something natural, but rather of people who feel destined to be unproductive. God tells these people not to say, "Here I am, a dry tree." In other words, do not say, "I'm fruitless and barren." The Lord promises to give them a place in His house better than that of sons and daughters. He also promises to give them an everlasting name. This means a lineage and heritage that will carry their name and cause them to be remembered. The Lord is promising to make the eunuchs fruitful.

In instructing eunuchs not to say they were a *dry tree*, God was proclaiming that they should not let their frustration over barrenness rule them. This is the way many people feel. They have a sense of the desire to be fruitful, yet they seem only frustrated. God is declaring, *I will release grace to you that will undo the Jezebel spirit that has sentenced you to fruitlessness. I will give you an everlasting heritage. Your destiny will not be one of barrenness, but one of productivity.*

Grace Empowers Fruitfulness

In the next chapters, we will discover how grace empowers us to be fruitful. Colossians 1:5–6 shows us the connection between grace and bearing fruit. Paul was telling the Colossian Church that he gave thanks and prayed for them "because of the hope which is laid up for you in heaven, of which you heard before in the word of the truth of the gospel, which has come to you, as it has also in all the world, and is bringing forth fruit, as it is also among you since the day you heard and knew the grace of God in truth."

Notice that *knowing the grace of God in truth* causes fruit to be born. It does this in all the world. This means whatever culture we might be in, it is the grace of God that empowers us to be fruitful. Fruitfulness is not the result of our superior wisdom or greater ability. Bearing fruit is the result of knowing the grace of God in truth.

In other words, when we have firsthand experience of God's grace and its effect on our lives, the result is the empowering of God that allows us to produce fruit. Frustration is lifted, inadequacy is removed and we begin to live the life of purpose we always knew we were meant for. So let's not just learn ideas about grace. Let's allow the Spirit of grace Himself, the Holy Spirit, to impart God's graciousness into our lives. Then we will become fruitful and fulfill the destiny of God for our future.

TWO

The Look of God

Throughout my history, I have listened as many preachers have sought to describe grace. Some have presented many good and beneficial ideas. Some have tried to reduce grace down to a few simple statements. This usually leaves much unexplained and unexplored. For instance, we probably all have heard that grace is *God's unmerited favor*. This is true, but is very limited in terms of what I understand grace to be in my spirit. Maybe you have also heard the acronym G.R.A.C.E. that is preached and taught as standing for *God's Resources At Christ's Expense*. Again, this is a good idea and is right, to a degree. It leaves much unexplained, however, that in my opinion would be part of a good living definition of grace.

Still others seem to think that grace is only about getting people saved so they can go to heaven when they die. They seem to have no concept of the role grace plays in our journey after the moment when Jesus comes into our lives as Savior. Sometimes grace is just preached as a theological idea we must simply accept by faith. Grace should not be just a theological concept, but should be a spiritual experience. If grace does not actually manifest in a real day-to-day experience for us, then I believe we have yet to discover the real grace of the God of the Bible.

Another issue is that many seem to believe grace is relegated only to the New Testament. They seem to think that God only became a God of grace after the Old Testament. Nothing could be further from the truth. For instance, the Old Testament declares God to be gracious. Exodus 33:19 shows Him declaring to Moses, "I will make all My goodness pass before you, and I will proclaim the name of the LORD before you. I will be gracious to whom I will be gracious, and I will have compassion on whom I will have compassion."

The word *gracious* from the Hebrew here is *chanan*. It means "to bend or stoop in kindness to an inferior." The Lord is declaring in the Old Testament that He is gracious. He is one who reaches to us in our inferior state. Isn't this what Paul said concerning Jesus in Romans 5:6–8?

> For when we were still without strength, in due time Christ died for the ungodly. For scarcely for a righteous man will one die; yet perhaps for a good man someone would even dare to die. But God demonstrates His own love toward us, in that while we were still sinners, Christ died for us.

As the image of God the Father, Jesus reached to us in our unredeemed state. When we were at our ugliest and most unlovable, Jesus died for us. God was in Him, bending and stooping to an inferior in kindness. God's nature did not change from the Old Testament to the New Testament. Through Jesus in the New Testament, God's nature was dramatically revealed. God's goodness was made manifest in the face of Jesus Christ.

Just as in the New Testament people saw the grace of God in the face of Jesus Christ, in the Old Testament there were those who also had this revelation of God's grace. Noah was one such man. The Bible makes some amazing statements about Noah and *why* he built an ark, to the saving of his house. Genesis 6:8 reveals the secret to Noah's salvation and that of his family: "But Noah found grace in the eyes of the LORD."

We can read this verse from the perspective that God decided to show Noah grace. Or we can read it from the perspective that through revelation, Noah understood the grace coming from the look of God. I believe through revelation, Noah saw the gracious nature of God that others were missing. As a result, he and his family received salvation that all the other parts of creation missed. The revelation of grace coming from the *look and eyes* of God did something in Noah's heart. The look or eyes of God being filled with grace speaks of the heart, demeanor and posture of God toward us. Noah became aware of the way God *saw* him. He had an understanding of the way the Lord perceived and thought about him.

When I say Noah *saw* the look of grace in God's eyes, I mean that he became aware of the attitude, desire and heart that God had toward him. This does not necessarily mean Noah actually saw the eyes of God. It does, however, mean Noah knew that God's heart toward him was one of love, acceptance and approval. God's heart toward us is not one of anger, destruction or judgment. God's heart toward us and His look at us are filled with grace, compassion and love.

How we *think God sees us* is imperative to how we live our life! Because Noah *saw* the grace that was in God's eyes, it brought salvation to him and his family that all others lost. The ones who could not see the grace in God's eyes perished in judgment. The same is true today. Only those who *see* the grace in God's eyes are saved. This means by revelation, we lose the idea of God being angry, upset and judgmental toward us. He instead has a different idea and position toward us. Our awareness of His posture of grace toward us creates faith in us to approach Him properly.

The Love behind the Look

Scripture says several things about what is *toward* us, or the *look of God toward* us. For instance, Romans 5:8 tells us that God's love is toward us: "But God demonstrates His own love toward us, in that while we were still sinners, Christ died for us." When Jesus died, it was the demonstration of God's love toward us. It was the look of grace in God's eyes. It was God in His gracious nature as our superior bending, reaching and stooping to us as the inferior. What an amazing thing to realize that God's look toward us is not one of disdain and disgust, but one of love, acceptance and desire.

Ephesians 1:7–9 also tells us of what is *toward* us from God, or what is in the look in His eyes:

> In Him we have redemption through His blood, the forgiveness of sins, according to the riches of His grace which He made to abound toward us in all wisdom and prudence, having made known to us the mystery of His will, according to His good pleasure which He purposed in Himself.

Notice that the riches of His grace, which bring forgiveness and redemption, are abounding toward us. They are His look toward us. God's grace is abounding toward us. He is not tolerating us or just putting up with us. He is actually excited about us. When we get this, it changes everything about the way we approach God and believe in Him. Condemnation, shame and guilt are removed. Many people I know live a life beset by guilt, which births fear. This is what the apostle Paul was contending against in his writings. From the revelation of justification by faith, Paul desired that we would know that God accepts us because of who Jesus is and what He has done and is doing. In Romans 8:31–35, the apostle seeks to reiterate these marvelous concepts and ideas:

> What then shall we say to these things? If God is for us, who can be against us? He who did not spare His own Son, but delivered Him up for us all, how shall He not with Him also freely give us all things? Who shall bring a charge against God's elect? It is God who justifies. Who is he who condemns? It is Christ who died, and furthermore is also risen, who is even at the right hand of God, who also makes intercession for us. Who shall separate us from the love of Christ? Shall tribulation, or distress, or persecution, or famine, or nakedness, or peril, or sword?

Paul seeks to free us from condemnation and any charge or indictment against us. He seeks to remind us that if God is for us, then who or what can stand against us and speak against us? God has justified us through the activity of His Son, Jesus, on the cross. This means there is no longer a word against us that can stand. Nothing can separate us from God's love. Not only is this true because of what Jesus has done, but also because of what He is presently doing through His intercession on our behalf. This is His grace at work. When we, through repentance and faith, accept what Jesus has done for us, this becomes a reality. We begin to see the way God is *looking* at us. This should produce great boldness and confidence. It should free us from the condemnation and guilt that want to hold us captive and pull us back into sinful activities.

This is what Jesus did for the woman caught in adultery in John 8:10–11. When His words had brought conviction on all those who had wanted to stone her, He then found Himself alone with her:

> When Jesus had raised Himself up and saw no one but the woman, He said to her, "Woman, where are those accusers of yours? Has no one condemned you?"
> She said, "No one, Lord."
> And Jesus said to her, "Neither do I condemn you; go and sin no more."

When Jesus asked her where her accusers were and if anyone condemned her, how freeing it must have been for her to say, "No one, Lord." Jesus had risen to defend her. When it seemed her fate was sealed and there awaited nothing but sure death from her sin, Jesus liberated her. He then made a powerful statement: "Neither do I condemn you; go and sin no more." With those words, Jesus freed this woman from the shame and guilt associated with her sin. The freedom from condemnation empowered her to go and sin no more.

This is always the case. Shame does not motivate us to righteousness and holiness. Shame will consistently pull us back into our sin. Shame makes us think less of ourselves than who and what we really are. We then begin to live out what we see ourselves to be. When Jesus declared this woman free from condemnation, however, He changed her identity and her perspective of who she was. From this new identity and the new way she saw herself, she could go and sin no more.

When we are forgiven and freed from condemnation, we are empowered to live above sin. The problem is that people think shame is a proper motivator, when in reality it is a devourer. Jeremiah 3:24–25 reveals that shame undealt with will devour us and even devour our lineage and labors:

> For shame has devoured the labor of our fathers from our youth—their flocks and their herds, their sons and their daughters. We lie down in our shame, and our reproach covers us. For we have sinned against the LORD our God, we and our fathers, from our youth even to this day, and have not obeyed the voice of the LORD our God.

Here we see shame devouring, and the passage mentions "the labor of our fathers from our youth." In other words, shame was fashioning people from their youth so that they could not properly steward the inheritance from their fathers. Shame will cause us to lose our inheritance because of the way we see ourselves. It causes us to make wrong decisions that result in inheritances being lost. We must see the *look* in God's eyes toward us. It is not one of condemnation and rejection, but of love and acceptance. When we see this, any shame leveled at us from parents or other sources can be undone. We can begin to see ourselves differently. We are not trash; we are treasured by the Lord.

It is impossible to bring people into holiness without a change of identity. When we demand that people live a certain way before they see themselves that way, it is called legalism. If, however, they begin to see themselves as God sees them from His *eyes*, it is now life giving and overcoming. The Scripture we just read from Jeremiah 3 mentions flocks and herds. This is speaking of the people of God. Elsewhere, Scripture refers to us as the sheep of His pasture (see Psalm 79:13). The truth is, the Church is being eaten up with shame, when actually we are valuable and precious in God's eyes. We must have a revelation of the way God is presently *seeing* us, and of the *look* in His eyes.

Jeremiah 3 also mentions sons and daughters being devoured by shame. Many people are losing their future and destiny because shame is consuming them. We must establish both natural children and spiritual children in their proper identity, free from shame. The passage also tells us that we "lie down in our shame." In other words, shame devours motivation. When shame causes us to believe the wrong things about ourselves, it steals away all motivation. We lose our initiative, and our drive is removed. Only when shame is removed can we again believe we have a future. This comes from seeing the way God is *seeing* us.

The other thing that comes from devouring shame is that we are caught in sinful patterns and habits. Jeremiah declared that the people had been held in sinful activity from their youth, even they and their fathers. This is what shame does. This is what Jesus freed the woman caught in adultery from. It was when He lifted shame and guilt from her that she was free to go and sin no more. What a powerful experience of freedom and forgiveness.

We find one more thing concerning what is *toward* us, or the way God is *seeing* us and the *look* in His eyes toward us, in Ephesians 2:7–9. God in His mercy made us alive, raised us up and seated us in heavenly places so that "in the ages to come He might show the exceeding riches of His grace in His kindness toward us in Christ Jesus. For by grace you have been saved through faith, and that not of yourselves; it is the gift of God, not of works, lest anyone should boast." God's kindness is *toward* us presently, and will also be toward us in the ages to come. The grace of God that is in His eyes toward us is not just for now. It does not run out. God is not going to change His mind about us. His attitude and posture toward us will last perpetually, for the ages to come. God is going to use us to demonstrate for the ages to come the greatness of His grace.

Ephesians 1:5–6 speaks of the praise of the glory of God's grace "having predestined us to adoption as sons by Jesus Christ to Himself, according to the good pleasure of His will, to the praise of the glory of His grace, by which He made us accepted in the Beloved." Only by revelation can we recognize how great the grace of God is. Because of His grace, we are "accepted in the Beloved" and are not rejected. God even predestined us out of His grace to the adoption of sons. This does not mean we do not have choice. We do. It means that all of heaven from the past, in the present and even the future is working on our behalf to bring us fully into all we were made for. This is the amazing grace of God at work. Should anyone ever question the goodness, kindness and graciousness of God, we will be His answer to them!

Faith to Embrace the Grace

The grace we have and will continue to operate in, now and for the ages to come, is apprehended by faith. Even this, however, comes from the Lord. He gives us the gift of faith to be able to embrace His grace. We will be totally an exhibition of the graciousness of who He is. This is why in Revelation

4:9–11, the twenty-four elders sitting on their thrones fall down and cast their crowns before Him:

> Whenever the living creatures give glory and honor and thanks to Him who sits on the throne, who lives forever and ever, the twenty-four elders fall down before Him who sits on the throne and worship Him who lives forever and ever, and cast their crowns before the throne, saying:
> "You are worthy, O Lord, to receive glory and honor and power; for You created all things, and by Your will they exist and were created."

As the four living creatures unveil the majesty of who God is in heaven, these twenty-four elders are compelled at this revelation to fall down and throw their crowns before His throne. They begin to worship Him with a proclamation of how worthy He is to be praised.

Crowns are the rewards for a life well lived in the earth. There are crowns of lovingkindness and mercy (see Psalm 103:4). There are crowns of glory and honor (see Psalm 8:5). There are crowns that are incorruptible (see 1 Corinthians 9:25). There are crowns of rejoicing (see 1 Thessalonians 2:19). There are crowns of righteousness (see 2 Timothy 4:8). There is a crown of life (see James 1:12). There are crowns of glory (see 1 Peter 5:4). The crowns these twenty-four elders are wearing as they sit on their thrones are crowns of gold. Revelation 4:4 shows them in their seated place of authority and function in heaven: "Around the throne were twenty-four thrones, and on the thrones I saw twenty-four elders sitting, clothed in white robes; and they had crowns of gold on their heads."

I understand these elders to be those from the earthen realm who have won positions of great influence in heaven.

They wear crowns and are clothed in white linen, which is the righteousness of the saints (see Revelation 19:8). It would be appropriate, therefore, to believe that the ones who sit on these thrones have been rewarded for their faithfulness while in the earth.

As the glory and majesty of God is decreed in heaven from revelation, these twenty-four fall down and cast the crowns they have won out of their obedience. Through this activity, they are acknowledging that the only reason they occupy their places is because of God's grace. They realize their power to obey did not come from themselves, but rather from Him who sits on the throne. This is not saying that God violates our free will. We *always* have the right to choose. From the influence of God's grace, however, the desire to serve and obey Him is worked into our very nature. This is why we become a *new creation*, carrying His desires in our heart. The casting of the elders' crowns is returning to Him the praise and acknowledgment of His glorious grace that allowed and empowered them to obey! It is all of His grace. We must see this in His eyes, as Noah did. It changes everything.

The Look That Unlocks Hope

One more thing I would mention about the grace that is in God's eyes is the *look* Jesus gave Peter after his denial. Luke 22:59–62 shows Peter denying the Lord, just as Jesus had told him he would do. As Peter denied that he knew Jesus, the rooster crowed:

> Then after about an hour had passed, another confidently affirmed, saying, "Surely this fellow also was with Him, for he is a Galilean."

But Peter said, "Man, I do not know what you are saying!"
Immediately, while he was still speaking, the rooster
crowed. And the Lord turned and looked at Peter. Then Peter
remembered the word of the Lord, how He had said to him,
"Before the rooster crows, you will deny Me three times."
So Peter went out and wept bitterly.

What must this moment have been like for Peter? He had
declared confidently that he would die with and for the
Lord. Yet when push came to shove, Peter's cowardice was
revealed. As the rooster crowed after his denial, Jesus turned
and looked at him. What was in this *look* that Jesus gave
Peter at this moment? What was in Jesus' *look* that broke
Peter's heart and changed him forever? Was it a look of anger
at being denied after all Jesus had done for him? Was it a
look of being upset and hurt at Peter's inability to stay true?
Was it a look of absolute disgust at Peter's rejection? Was it
a look of deep disappointment in the one whom Jesus had
poured so much time into? What was the look Peter saw in
the eyes of Jesus at this moment?

It was none of these I have mentioned. The look Peter
saw in Jesus' eyes was one of absolute love, acceptance and
remembrance of their history together. It was a look of grace
in the midst of Peter's denial, as Jesus assured Peter of His
love and commitment to him. This look broke Peter's heart.
This is what grace does. First John 4:19 tells us our empowerment to love the Lord flows out of His love for us: "We
love Him because He first loved us." The love of the Lord
toward us extracts our love and commitment to Him. This
is what was happening with Peter. This is why he wept so
bitterly. The love and grace he encountered in this one look
from Jesus unveiled his heart. He saw from Jesus' look his

own unworthiness of this kind of love, yet Jesus was giving it to him.

This love and grace in the eyes of Jesus reached deep into Peter's heart. So it also does in our hearts. When we by faith see the grace that is in God's eyes, the grace that we are completely unworthy of, it changes us. This grace and love reaches deep inside us and begins to create the very nature of God in us.

Usually, there is first a deep brokenness that results from this kind of encounter. God's look brings us to the end of ourselves and any confidence we have in our flesh. We look at ourselves and realize there is nothing good in us. Lest this seems too hard, we must realize that anything good in us is from the Lord. We must stop our flattery of ourselves and allow Jesus' look of grace to unveil us.

There is actually no more precious place than these places of deep brokenness created by the look of grace in Jesus' eyes. Paul said this in Romans 7:18: "For I know that in me (that is, in my flesh) nothing good dwells; for to will is present with me, but how to perform what is good I do not find." Paul was declaring that he wanted to do right and good, but he did not find the power to do it in himself. He recognized that he needed a Savior who could change this.

Peter realized this same thing, probably for the first time, when Jesus looked at him with the eyes of grace. Simultaneously, however, Jesus' look unlocked hope for Peter's future—that even though he had failed miserably, Jesus was committed to redeeming him. Why would anyone be willing to do this? Only because of the graciousness within. Peter may have been tempted to second-guess the look he saw in Jesus' eyes. Maybe he wondered for a moment if it were just the weariness and fatigue from the beating Jesus had endured. If, however, the look of grace in Jesus' eyes was going to have its impact, Peter would have to believe what he had seen and perceived. Jesus did still love him, in spite of his denial.

We, too, must believe what the Word of God declares, but also what we perceive from the Spirit of truth. Jesus does love us. God is on our side. If we will believe what we have seen in His eyes, we can escape the corruption that is in the world through lust (see 2 Peter 1:4). We can be transformed into God's image and likeness, even as by the Spirit of the Lord (see 2 Corinthians 3:18). The grace that is in the eyes of the Lord will not only deliver us from judgment; it will also secure us for His eternal Kingdom. We will be living demonstrations of the goodness of His grace. He will finish that which He began in us.

THREE

Seeking Mercy, Finding Grace

Grace does not just cause us to be forgiven. Grace actually allows us to become possessors of our inheritance. Let's look at the idea behind this concept. You are probably familiar with the story of the Prodigal Son recorded in Luke 15. In this story of a man with two sons, the younger asks for his inheritance and the father grants it to him. This son then leaves the family home and travels into a faraway land, where he wastes the inheritance. After this, he finds himself feeding pigs just to survive. At this point, the Bible says he comes to his senses. He decides he will go home and ask to be treated like one of his father's hired servants. We pick up the young man's story in Luke 15:15–24:

> Then he went and joined himself to a citizen of that country, and he sent him into his fields to feed swine. And he would gladly have filled his stomach with the pods that the swine ate, and no one gave him anything.
>
> But when he came to himself, he said, "How many of my father's hired servants have bread enough and to spare, and I

perish with hunger! I will arise and go to my father, and will say to him, 'Father, I have sinned against heaven and before you, and I am no longer worthy to be called your son. Make me like one of your hired servants.'"

And he arose and came to his father. But when he was still a great way off, his father saw him and had compassion, and ran and fell on his neck and kissed him. And the son said to him, "Father, I have sinned against heaven and in your sight, and am no longer worthy to be called your son."

But the father said to his servants, "Bring out the best robe and put it on him, and put a ring on his hand and sandals on his feet. And bring the fatted calf here and kill it, and let us eat and be merry; for this my son was dead and is alive again; he was lost and is found." And they began to be merry.

One of the main things that stands out in this story is that the boy was intent on asking his father for mercy. His only request was that he just be made like one of the household servants. He felt his sin was so great that he could never be a *son* again. But he underestimated the heart of his father. The moment he began his prepared speech about becoming a servant, his father interrupted him and called for a robe, ring and sandals. He called for the fatted calf to be killed and a party to take place. The father was anything but aggravated or impatient toward his wayward son. In fact, he completely restored him to his place in the household and gave him his inheritance as a son back. The boy was going to ask for mercy, but the father gave him grace.

Mercy will forgive us for our sin so we do not receive retribution for it. Grace, on the other hand, restores us to our position, or maybe even to a position we never had. Mercy is good, but grace is beyond comprehension. In this story, Jesus was communicating the goodness and graciousness of the Father. None of His listeners yet had an awareness of it. They knew God was merciful, but who had ever heard of a God who would not only forgive sin, but also let it have no lasting effect against us?

Grace Misunderstood

The elder brother in this Prodigal Son story, however, is a picture of most of us. He is a picture of not understanding the difference between the God who shows mercy and the God who gives grace. This elder brother became angry because of his father's graciousness. Luke 15:25–32 shows us his response when he hears of the graciousness extended to his younger brother:

> Now his older son was in the field. And as he came and drew near to the house, he heard music and dancing. So he called one of the servants and asked what these things meant. And he said to him, "Your brother has come, and because he has received him safe and sound, your father has killed the fatted calf."
>
> But he was angry and would not go in. Therefore his father came out and pleaded with him. So he answered and said to his father, "Lo, these many years I have been serving you; I never transgressed your commandment at any time; and yet you never gave me a young goat, that I might make merry with my friends. But as soon as this son of yours came, who has devoured your livelihood with harlots, you killed the fatted calf for him."
>
> And he said to him, "Son, you are always with me, and all that I have is yours. It was right that we should make merry and be glad, for your brother was dead and is alive again, and was lost and is found."

This is a picture of the people of God who do not understand grace themselves. The older brother probably would have had no problem with the father showing mercy to the younger brother. The problem was the grace he was receiving. If the younger had mercifully been allowed to live in the servants' quarters and eat the servants' rations, there would have been no problem. It was the fact that the father graciously threw a party and killed the calf that was reserved for something important. He put clean clothes on this returned son and restored his position. This is what was beyond the comprehension of the older son.

The truth is, neither son understood the grace of the father. The younger, who needed forgiveness and restoration, did not. Neither did the older, who stayed at home and never went anywhere. Only in the midst of terrible failure was grace manifested. This is why Romans 5:20 makes the statement it does about the marvels of grace: "Moreover the law entered that the offense might abound. But where sin abounded, grace abounded much more . . ."

This is quite an amazing statement. The greater the sin, the more grace available. This is because the goodness of God is magnified in the midst of the greatest failures. We do not get this. It is hard for us to compute. No matter how big the sin might be, there is a grace that is bigger. Not just a grace to forgive, but also a grace to restore and give destiny, just as if the sin had never happened.

I remember a great teacher of God's Word explaining it this way: Perhaps a bank employee steals a lot of money. He is found out. He repents. The bank's authorities decide they will show him mercy and not charge or prosecute him. He is, of course, relieved of his duties and can no longer work for the bank, but he has just received mercy. That alone is amazing. He will feel very grateful and will rejoice that he is not going to jail and his family is not being left destitute. He has been spared.

But what if the bank authorities, along with forgiving him and not prosecuting him, allowed him to keep his job? *Unthinkable!* And what if it did not end there? What if they not only allowed him to keep his job, but also promoted him to bank president?

What? He has just received grace. This is *amazing grace*. This is what manifests the goodness of God in such a way that it gets the attention of the Church and the world.

We would say, "But there should be some consequences to his sin."

The answer is, *"Grace!"*

Because we do not understand grace when it occurs, we can be like the older son. We struggle with grace because of how good God is. Where sin abounds, grace does *much more* abound. We must have our mind renewed to think from a *grace* mindset. Otherwise, we end up condemning people whom God is not condemning. This is what Jesus referred to in Matthew 12:7: "But if you had known what this means, 'I desire mercy and not sacrifice,' you would not have condemned the guiltless."

Jesus was saying, "Because you don't understand the true gracious nature of the Father, you keep condemning those God isn't condemning." What a powerful statement. Our lack of understanding of grace makes us condemning, judgmental and condescending people. We leave little or no room for others' mistakes and redemption. All because we do not understand how good God is to those who repent and turn to Him. There is nothing that cannot be forgiven, along with restoration being brought, to those who by faith *reach for*

His grace. His grace not only frees us from the consequences of sin; it launches us into our ultimate destiny, purpose and inheritance.

This is what happened to this young son. To his utter shock and amazement, his father was more good than he had ever realized, even though he had lived in his father's house from birth. How often this happens today. God's people who know Him have *lived* in the Father's house, the Church, and still do not know how good He is. This is because the preaching of grace has been insufficient in the Church. It seems that quite often, the Church either tends toward legalism or leans toward easy, greasy grace. Both are in error, in my opinion. Legalism brings arrogance and death. Paul was clear in 2 Corinthians 3:5–6 that the law or the letter brings death to all who try to be righteous by keeping it: "Our sufficiency is from God, who also made us sufficient as ministers of the new covenant, not of the letter but of the Spirit; for the letter kills, but the Spirit gives life."

None are able to keep the law. Those who think they can, or who think they are keeping the law, will invariably become arrogant and haughty. Those who fail to keep it will wither under the power of shame. We do not have the ability to keep God's standard, apart from the empowerment of the Holy Spirit. The Holy Spirit will lead us into the righteous standard of God for our life. (We will get into this more later.) We as the Church need to teach a well-balanced view of God's grace and how it really operates in the believer's life. Without a true understanding of grace, we produce believers who are defeated and incapable of living the kind of life Jesus has provided for us. Condemnation destroys the destiny God had for them through a sense of constant unworthiness besetting them.

Still others teach a grace where there are no consequences to sin, even without repentance. They teach that the grace of God we received at salvation is enough for us, regardless of the kind of lives we live. Some even go so far as to teach the *gospel of inclusion* where *all* are saved, no matter whether they repent or not. I am desperately against these ideas and am afraid they could be sentencing millions to the horrors of hell in the afterlife. I often say concerning those who espouse this kind of grace that they had better hope they are right. Otherwise, their teaching will result in myriads being eternally tormented and lost.

Coming Back to Grace

The grace I believe the Church must teach is the grace found through faith and repentance. This is what happened to the Prodigal Son. He received grace even though he only sought mercy. Notice that he received it only after some activity and effort on his part. Let me mention the things he did that allowed him to receive grace. The first thing he did was *he came to himself*. In other words, he came to the realization of his situation. It is amazing how deceptive sin can be. We are told in Hebrews 3:13 that sin has a hardening and deceptive effect: "But exhort one another daily, while it is called 'Today,' lest any of you be hardened through the deceitfulness of sin."

It is amazing how deceived we can be in regard to our condition. Sin deceives us and makes us think we are okay, or that our future is okay. When the young man came to himself, the blinders caused by his sin came off. He saw the place he was in and how bad it was. This is called the *conviction of the Holy Spirit*. This is when we recognize and become brutally honest about ourselves. None of us can come to this place without the Holy Spirit bringing us there.

The conviction of the Holy Spirit is a gift from God, even though in the moment it is very unpleasant. The Holy Spirit causes sin to appear exceedingly sinful. He uses the law or standard of God to make sin really appear as what it is. Paul referred to this in Romans 7:13: "Has then what is good become death to me? Certainly not! But sin, that it might appear sin, was producing death in me through what is good, so that sin through the commandment might become exceedingly sinful."

God allowed sin through the commandment to produce death in us. This is what happened to the Prodigal. He came to himself. He was now ready to take action to change his course and destiny. He came to a conclusion and realized something had to change. Better yet, he realized that he had to change.

The next thing he did was *he came up with a proposition* for his father. He knew that he was at the mercy of his father, who could reject him and not allow him back into the house. This son was in a very humbling place. He was not coming to demand something from the father; he was intent on pleading for mercy from him. This must be our posture as well in order to receive grace. When we are guilty of sin, we need the acceptance of the Father to work for us. When David was guilty of sin with Bathsheba and the murder of Uriah, he knew he was at God's mercy. He did not have a leg to stand on. Psalm 51:1–4 shows us David pleading with God for mercy:

> Have mercy upon me, O God, according to Your loving-kindness; according to the multitude of Your tender mercies,

blot out my transgressions. Wash me thoroughly from my iniquity, and cleanse me from my sin.

For I acknowledge my transgressions, and my sin is always before me. Against You, You only, have I sinned, and done this evil in Your sight—that You may be found just when You speak, and blameless when You judge.

David acknowledged his transgressions before God. He acknowledged that even though he had dealt treacherously with others, God was the one true Judge and would Himself determine David's fate. He asked for mercy. We must lay aside every sense of being owed anything. We must humble ourselves before the Lord and ask for His mercy. This is what the young son did as he planned his return to his father's house.

Another thing the Prodigal did was he then *arose* and came to his father. This speaks of getting ourselves out of the situation we are in. Real repentance has action attached to it. I remember years ago having a dream where Jesus came to me. In the dream He told me, *You have grieved the Father.* I understood this to be from the Lord. Jesus acts as our advocate with the Father (see 1 John 2:1). Jesus was coming to me in my dream, advocating for me from the Father. When Jesus spoke those words in my dream, I knew what I had done, what had caused me to do it and what I needed to do to correct it. I did, in fact, do these things in response to the dream. I *arose*. I did not just say some words of repentance. I ordered my steps in agreement with what I needed to change.

This is what Paul spoke of in Romans 13:14, "But put on the Lord Jesus Christ, and make no provision for the flesh, to fulfill its lusts." To make no provision for the flesh means that I control my circumstances as much as I can. I do not put myself in places where the temptation is there. I keep myself away from those situations. This is what I did in response to the dream. I was arising and removing myself from the place where temptation could come and I would sin. The young man in the story arose and went home. As soon as the father saw him, he had compassion on him. He ran and fell on his neck and kissed him, welcoming him home. I am sure the Prodigal must have been flabbergasted at this. He clearly did not think this was the welcome he would receive. Yet here was his father, showing nothing but mercy, kindness and grace.

It is quite interesting that the father never once made a move to go after the son, until the son made a move to come home. This *arising* is what releases grace. The father clearly loved his son and wanted him back. He knew, however, that it had to be the son's decision to return. When we *come back* to the Father, there awaits grace for us. But we must do the turning. James 4:8 gives us the admonition to take the first step back to God: "Draw near to God and He will draw near to you. Cleanse your hands, you sinners; and purify your hearts, you double-minded."

We are told that when we come near to the Lord by cleansing our hands of sin and purifying any double-mindedness from our hearts, God comes to us. This Prodigal Son had made up his mind to come home. He did not say to himself, *If my dad does this or this, I will stay.* No! He knew he was wrong, and he was ready to accept whatever was meted out to him. Again, to his utter surprise he found a father so gracious that it was unbelievable. As the boy began his prepared speech of unworthiness, his father interrupted him. It was as if his father did not even hear what his son was saying, for the joy that he had returned. His returning was more important to the father than his words.

Words are easy. They are necessary, but easy. Actions and humility are hard. The father was aware of what it had taken for his son to come home. This was enough repentance for him. He did not require his son to grovel or beg. He could see the repentance in him. The boy had not eaten, and I am sure he looked nothing like he had looked back when he left home. He was thin and scraggly. He probably smelled like the pigs he had been feeding. None of this turned the father away.

Repositioned by Grace

I have often said that when we receive prodigals back, we must not be offended by the smell of the pigs on them. This father was not repelled. He was so happy to have his son home. He called for four things as he released grace, and not just mercy, to his son. He first said to bring the best robe. The word *robe* in the Greek is *stole*, which carries the meaning of "a gown that is a mark of dignity"! The first thing the father did was restore this young man's dignity by clothing him. The Bible says it was the "best robe," which means it was the most important one. The father reinstated the young man with a sense of importance. Dignity came again into his spirit. He began to have an awareness of how important he was to his father and his house.

When we receive grace, dignity comes again into our spirit. We are *not* sinners saved by grace. We are the righteousness of God in Christ Jesus because of grace. This young man was set again into sonship. The apostle John speaks of this sense of dignity in 1 John 3:1: "Behold what manner of love the

Father has bestowed on us, that we should be called children of God! Therefore the world does not know us, because it did not know Him." The love of the Father firmly testifies to our worth and dignity. We must accept this and believe it. This is what grace brings to us.

The second thing the father called for was a ring to be placed on the Prodigal's finger. The ring in that culture was not a vanity thing or a decorative item. The ring said the son had power of attorney. He was being established in a place of honor and authority. Because he wore the ring, he had the right to make decisions on behalf of the father. This was a place of great trust and significance. This was grace at work. This boy was not settled into the household as a servant, as he requested. He was esteemed again as a son in the house, with full rights and power.

Third, the father then called for sandals to be placed on the boy's feet. Servants wore no sandals; only heirs in the house wore them. By placing sandals on his son, the father was making a statement that he was restored to full status as a son. He was not a mere servant. The father wanted his son to recognize who he was, but he also wanted those from outside the house to know who he was. When the son had asked for his inheritance before the time, it had been a rebellious and shameful act. The father had most likely had to sell a portion of his estate to give the son what he asked. This would have become a point of gossip in the community. In calling for the robe, ring and sandals, the father was making a statement for all to see. This was his *son*, and he was proud of him and fully accepted him in this place in the house. The father was willing to accept all the ridicule and gossip associated with receiving the Prodigal home. He was just so excited to have him back.

The fourth and last thing the father did was kill that fatted calf and throw a party. I like to say that the father had begun to fatten up the calf the day his rebellious son left, in anticipation of his return. This father was living for the day when this son would come home. When the son returned, the calf was butchered and the house and community had a party in honor of the returned prodigal. We could understand throwing a party for a hero or someone who has accomplished something significant. Throwing a party for a college graduate or someone who has finished another task would make sense to us. But who throws a party for a rebellious son who has wasted his livelihood and comes home in shame, smelling like pigs? The answer is, only the Father of all grace and goodness. He values us so very much. If we could only understand His love toward us, we would come home to Him in humility, but with great confidence that we would be loved, accepted and forgiven.

What a wonderful Father we have. What an expression of grace we have received. The Prodigal was prepared to ask for mercy, but instead received grace. So it is with us. The love of the Father and His house will do the necessary work in us that will cause us never to stray again. When we come in humility, faith and repentance, God our Father is free to do the unthinkable for us. He reveals His kindness, and we become recipients of His graciousness and love. May the grace of our Father work mightily in us. From this grace, we are empowered to live as overcomers and as those who will declare the praise of this glorious grace now and forever.

FOUR

Grace versus Works

As we talk of grace and seek to explain it in light of God's heart toward us, we must deal with what the Bible calls *works*. As good evangelicals, we would all tout the expression "we are saved by grace and not works." This is taken from Ephesians 2:8–9, "For by grace you have been saved through faith, and that not of yourselves; it is the gift of God, not of works, lest anyone should boast." What a powerful statement the apostle Paul makes. This came from revelation that came to Paul while he was set aside in the wilderness. After his conversion on the road to Damascus, he spent considerable time in the wilderness, where God brought him a revelation of His grace and salvation. Paul was explicit about not having learned or received this revelation from a person. He declared that it had come from personal visitations with the Lord through the Holy Spirit. We call this revelation the *justification by faith*.

In other words, we are not saved because our good works outweigh the bad. We are saved by grace alone. Notice that

Paul declares we are saved through a faith we did not generate. It was a gift from God. God gave us a gift to respond to the grace He was offering us. John 1:16–17 speaks of this: "And of His fullness we have all received, and grace for grace. For the law was given through Moses, but grace and truth came through Jesus Christ."

Moses brought the Law. Jesus brought a revelation of grace and truth. Scripture says we received of His fullness by receiving *grace* for *grace*. This is amazing. God gives us grace to be able to embrace grace. This is what I believe the apostle Paul was saying. We are given the gift of faith to embrace the grace being extended to us. This means our salvation is *all* from God. Our responsibility is simply to respond to what He is offering us. We do not initiate any of it. God is the initiator, and we are the responders.

If grace is extended to us and we reject it, this is where the trouble comes in. This is why people are lost and doomed to hell. It is because they have despised the gift of God and have not valued it. Hebrews 10:28–31 shows us the perils of rejecting the grace and faith God would extend to us:

> Anyone who has rejected Moses' law dies without mercy on the testimony of two or three witnesses. Of how much worse punishment, do you suppose, will he be thought worthy who has trampled the Son of God underfoot, counted the blood of the covenant by which he was sanctified a common thing, and insulted the Spirit of grace? For we know Him who said, "Vengeance is Mine, I will repay," says the Lord. And again, "The LORD will judge His people." It is a fearful thing to fall into the hands of the living God.

This Scripture is basically communicating that if we reject the goodness and grace of God, the penalty is severe. The writer's point is that if people died without mercy under an inferior covenant, what would be our penalty if we reject the gospel of grace? Because God does everything for us and only asks that we respond, the penalty is great if we despise His goodness and grace. The writer finishes this idea with the statement, "It is a fearful thing to fall into the hands of the living God." This is why we must labor to have soft and tender hearts before the Lord. This keeps us from rejecting the graciousness of His offers.

Even before New Testament times, God preached the gospel of grace to Abraham. Abraham discovered that what the Lord wanted was a believing person. Galatians 3:6–9 shows us that even though Abraham lived in Old Testament times, he lived from New Testament revelation. This is what made him so powerful and enabled him to live outside the limitation that was set on others. The power for Abraham to live a life that is still affecting the world today came out of his revelation of justification being by faith and not by works and performance. It was God's grace in and on Abraham that produced this empowerment:

> Abraham "believed God, and it was accounted to him for righteousness." Therefore know that only those who are of faith are sons of Abraham. And the Scripture, foreseeing that God would justify the Gentiles by faith, preached the gospel to Abraham beforehand, saying, "In you all the nations shall be blessed." So then those who are of faith are blessed with believing Abraham.

When we forsake the works of the law and exercise faith, as Abraham did, we become the sons and seed of Abraham. The same realms he lived from and in, we have access into as well. Even though he was an Old Testament man, Abraham lived in the grace of a New Testament believer because of faith. He understood that it is not works that get us benefits from God; it is grace. It is so very easy to place our confidence in our own efforts. Abraham discovered this was not the secret. Romans 4:1–4 gives us clues into what he found out:

> What then shall we say that Abraham our father has found according to the flesh? For if Abraham was justified by works, he has something to boast about, but not before God. For what does the Scripture say? "Abraham believed God, and it was accounted to him for righteousness." Now to him who works, the wages are not counted as grace but as debt.

The passage here asks what Abraham found. As he walked with God, he discovered some new things. He probably also discovered that some of the former things he had thought about God were untrue. There were probably things he did not believe about God that he would come to believe. One of the main things he *found* was that getting things from God, and pleasing Him, was not accomplished through works meant to impress Him. What impressed God was faith. As I heard a fellow teacher and preacher say, "God's greatest pain is to be doubted. However, God's greatest pleasure is to be believed." When we doubt God, it bogs everything down. When we believe Him, it accelerates everything. Abraham discovered this.

Notice please that Paul speaks of making God our debtor. When we perform well, we expect a payday from the Lord. For instance, if you work forty hours, you expect your employer to give you a paycheck. Your work and time have, in essence, made him or her your debtor. If the employer does not pay, you can file a grievance and even win a judgment. We do this same thing to God, if we are not careful. We say our prayers, pay our tithes, attend services, try to walk holy, and think this requires God to respond. We think God *owes* us because of our *works*. Abraham found out that this is not the way God operates. He will not be our debtor. We cannot hold Him for ransom. What God responds to is a faith that lays hold of His grace.

Through faith we believe in God's goodness and graciousness to us, based on what His Son, Jesus, has done for us. Our faith is in His goodness, not in our own works of righteousness. Romans 5:1–2 shows us that we have access into grace through faith: "Therefore, having been justified by faith, we have peace with God through our Lord Jesus Christ, through whom also we have access by faith into this grace in which we stand, and rejoice in hope of the glory of God." We are justified by faith and have access into His grace. When we exercise faith in the goodness of God, this is what He responds to.

It is not a confidence in our works, but a confidence in His. Galatians 2:16 makes a profound statement concerning the futility of our own works:

> Knowing that a man is not justified by the works of the law but by faith in Jesus Christ, even we have believed in Christ Jesus, that we might be justified by faith in Christ and not by the works of the law; for by the works of the law no flesh shall be justified.

"By the works of the law *no* flesh shall be justified" (emphasis added). We are justified and found blameless through faith in Jesus Christ and what He did for us on the cross, and also through His resurrection. I believe, however, that we get what is being declared here through repentance. Repentance is an act of faith. Peter was clear about the way remission of sins occurs. Acts 2:38 tells us that repentance, along with baptism, brings remission of sin and the empowerment of the Holy Spirit: "Then Peter said to them, 'Repent, and let every one of you be baptized in the name of Jesus Christ for the remission of sins; and you shall receive the gift of the Holy Spirit.'"

Some have read this and concluded that you cannot be saved without water baptism. I do not believe this. Romans 10:8–10 shows that confessing with our mouth as we believe in our heart produces salvation:

> But what does it say? "The word is near you, in your mouth and in your heart" (that is, the word of faith which we preach): that if you confess with your mouth the Lord Jesus and believe in your heart that God has raised Him from the dead, you will be saved. For with the heart one believes unto righteousness, and with the mouth confession is made unto salvation.

There is no mention of baptism here as far as securing salvation for the soul. I do, however, believe baptism is important to getting the fullness of grace available to us. When Peter said *repent*, that is what brought the remission of sins. When we repent we turn from ungodliness, but we also turn from our own efforts to be righteous. We are declaring, "My only hope is in the righteousness Jesus obtained for me."

When I am baptized, however, I am coming into alignment with heaven. I am identifying with the death of Jesus on my behalf, but also identifying by faith with His resurrected life. This is where the empowerment of the Holy Spirit comes in. My willingness to obey and come into God's order releases to me the fullness of His grace through the Holy Spirit. The Holy Spirit is the one who administers God's grace into my life. I am not saying that people always have to be water baptized before they become filled with the Holy Spirit. There are exceptions in Scripture where this is not so. When Peter said *repent and be baptized*, however, it is clear that repentance brings us remission of sin and baptism aligns us to receive the empowerment of the Spirit. These are not senseless religious acts. They are acts from faith that allow us to embrace the fullness of God's grace available to us. Remember that the Holy Spirit we receive is the Spirit of grace (see Hebrews 10:29).

The Seed of God in Us

Having declared that we are saved by grace and a confidence in God's works and not our own, we need to know that this does not exclude us from *good works*. In fact, the grace we receive *demands* good works from us. As some have declared, "We don't work for grace, but we do work from grace." Without question, Titus 2:11–14 shows that because we have received grace, we are pushed to holiness. If I have received the real grace of God into my life, the Holy Spirit will press me into new levels of holy living:

> For the grace of God that brings salvation has appeared to all men, teaching us that, denying ungodliness and worldly lusts, we should live soberly, righteously, and godly in the present age, looking for the blessed hope and glorious appearing of our great God and Savior Jesus Christ, who gave Himself for us, that He might redeem us from every lawless deed and purify for Himself His own special people, zealous for good works.

First, notice that this is the *grace* that brings salvation to all men. The real grace of God that produces salvation will create a longing and passion for holiness in us. This does not mean we live perfect lives and never fail. What it does mean is that when I blow it, I cannot live with myself until I deal with it and get it fixed. The grace of God in me will urge and catapult me toward a place of righteous living. We are told this grace *teaches* us how to live this way. The word *teach* in the Greek is *paideuo*. It means "to train up a child, to discipline." The grace of God in us will teach us progressively how to live in a godly manner. It will discipline and correct us progressively so that the divine nature in us can take the dominant role. The grace of God we received produces in us the divine nature of God.

First John 3:9 tells us that the *seed* of God is in us: "Whoever has been born of God does not sin, for His seed remains in him; and he cannot sin, because he has been born of God." This word in the Greek is *sperma*. It is speaking of "that which reproduces and causes conception." Scripture says this *seed remains* in us. This means that what we received at conversion through the grace of God is still in us, working. It is continually moving us toward the image of our Father, whose *seed* is in us. It is impossible for those truly born again and saved to live an unholy life and not be miserable. There is a divine nature we have received from God in us.

I like to illustrate it this way. There are times I put my reading glasses on to work on my computer. When the black screen shows up as the computer turns on, I see my reflection in it. As I am looking at myself with my reading glasses on, I wonder, *How did my dad get in my computer?* This is because I have become aware that at this stage in my life, I look progressively like my natural dad more and more. Why? Because his seed is in me. His sperm caused me to be conceived. In my earlier years I did not think I looked like my dad, but the older I become, the more I resemble him. Again, this is because his seed/nature is in me.

This is the way it happens to us spiritually as well. By grace we received the divine nature of God. The more mature we become in our spiritual walk, the more we reflect the Father's nature/seed in us. This is because the grace we received is constantly disciplining us to change the way we think, behave, act and respond. We become more like our Father because of the grace we received that brings salvation to all men.

Reckon the Realities of the Cross

Notice in Titus 2:12 that out of the grace we have received, we also *deny* ungodliness and worldly lust. This word *deny* means "to disavow and reject." We are empowered to say no to sin and its pull. Because of the grace we have received that forms the new nature of God in us, what we did not have power over before, we now do. Some people think they still have a sin nature working in them. Biblically speaking, this is not true. They think because they are tempted, it is the sign of a sin nature driving them toward sin. The fact is that when we accepted Jesus as our Savior and received the nature of God through His grace, the sin nature in us died.

Temptation is not the sign of a sin nature. Jesus did not have a sin nature, because He was born of the Holy Spirit. Yet He was tempted without sin (see Hebrews 4:15). The sign of having a sin nature is the inability to say no to sin. When we were born again, the power of sin over us was broken. It no longer rules over us when we, by faith, accept that which the cross of Jesus and His grace has done for us.

There are those who would teach that once you are born again, you now have two natures inside you. They would say you have the nature of God and your old sin nature simultaneously living in you. They then would say that the one you feed becomes the strongest. They would say if you feed or nurture the old sin nature through fleshly thinking and activities, then it grows and dominates you. If, however, you give yourself to spiritual things, the divine nature rules in you. This is *not* exactly right by biblical standards. The Bible calls this sin nature the *old man*, and Romans 6:6 gives us some insight into what the crucifixion of Jesus did with this *old man* or sin nature: "Our old man was crucified with Him, that the body of sin might be done away with, that we should no longer be slaves of sin."

The *old man* has died and is being done away with. There is a progressive removal of any influence it would have in us, as the grace of God works abundantly within. Years ago I had a dream that an old man was urinating and some of it was splashing upward on my head. I know that image is gross, but God was showing me something through this dream. He was letting me know that I was allowing the uncleanness of the *old man* to affect my thought life. I needed to take the authority I had as a believer and stop this from happening. I needed to *reckon* the realities of the cross effective in my life. Romans 6:11–12 tells us to aggressively, by faith, put into place the effects of the cross against the *old man*/sin nature: "Likewise you also, reckon yourselves to be dead indeed to sin, but alive to God in Christ Jesus our Lord. Therefore do not let sin reign in your mortal body, that you should obey it in its lusts."

Do not allow sin to rule and reign in you. Because of what Jesus did to it at the cross, it has no more power. The grace of God within you has caused the *old man* to die and the divine nature of God to live in you. The grace of God working in us strengthens us to resist temptation that we otherwise would give in to. The grace of God in us grants us the authority to live in a holy manner. We are able to live soberly, righteously and godly in this present evil world. The grace of God in us fashions us; we are no longer fashioned by the world or its systems. Because of God's grace, we are redeemed from every lawless deed and purified to be His own special people. He claims us because of His grace in us.

The Law of the Spirit of Life

The Holy Spirit as the Spirit of grace also works in this equation to cause us to live a life of *good works*. It is in our coming under the control of the Spirit of God, who functionally brings His grace, that we are set free from the law of works. Romans 8:1–4 gives us some astounding insight into the dynamics of being freed from the law and trying to gain our own righteousness:

> There is therefore now no condemnation to those who are in Christ Jesus, who do not walk according to the flesh, but according to the Spirit. For the law of the Spirit of life in Christ Jesus has made me free from the law of sin and death. For what the law could not do in that it was weak through the flesh, God did by sending His own Son in the likeness of sinful flesh, on account of sin: He condemned sin in the flesh, that the righteous requirement of the law might be fulfilled in us who do not walk according to the flesh but according to the Spirit.

Paul begins this discourse by declaring that there is "no condemnation" to whoever is in Christ Jesus. The reason for this is because the *law of the Spirit of life has set me free from the law of sin and death*. The law of sin and death basically says, "If you sin, you die." This is where condemnation comes from. We intuitively know that our sin makes us worthy of death. It makes us worthy of the death of our dreams, our future, our life and our eternity.

Jesus came in the flesh and broke the power of sin. Because of what He did, sin was judged and condemned. Paul then declared that as a result of this, we are free to fulfill the righteous requirement of the law. We do not keep the jot and tittle of the law. We actually fulfill what the law was after all the time. We fulfill the righteousness the law was seeking to bring. Because Jesus' death broke the power of sin, when we receive Him and His grace, we now have power over sin. We are free to fulfill what God was after through the law. We do this by coming under the *law of the Spirit of life*. We do not do it by being rule keepers. We do it by living under the authority of the Spirit of grace, which is the Spirit of life. We are removed from that which brings condemnation and placed under that which brings life.

Notice that we are freed from the *law* of sin and death and placed under the *law* of the Spirit of life. This is important. I have witnessed people trying to be free from the law of legalism, and they think they can do anything they desire. This is not true. I remember speaking at a conference years ago and then going back to a certain host's house to relax after the meeting. Only the speakers and a few handpicked people were invited. When we got to the house, there was drinking to the point of intoxication, coarse language and other activities that made me uncomfortable. It was not just what was being done; it was the *spirit* in which it was being done that concerned me. They felt themselves *free* to do these things. They felt *free* from "religion" and its oppressive effects. I sensed there was something in that setting that was not pleasing to the Lord. It was as if they were using their *liberty* for an occasion to the flesh. This is what Paul spoke of in Galatians 5:13: "For you, brethren, have been called to liberty; only do not use liberty as an opportunity for the flesh, but through love serve one another."

These people's excuse for what was happening was that they had been set free from religious restraints. They therefore could do such things without condemnation or guilt. This is wrong. This is not the real grace of God. To do this would make someone *lawless*. In other words, living without law. This is not what we are called to. We are called to come under the law of the Spirit of life, where the Holy Spirit dictates and determines our activities. Otherwise, we are living lawless and unaccountable lives. We begin to give in to the lust of the flesh, claiming we are free. This is deception. You can only come out from under the law of sin and death by coming under the law of the Spirit of life. This principle is espoused in other places in Scripture. Paul speaks of it again in Galatians 5:18, "But if you are led by the Spirit, you are not under the law."

When we surrender our lives under the authority and governance of the Spirit of God, we are no longer obligated to keep the law. We have come under another law. We are not lawless; we are under the power of the Spirit of God. The Holy Spirit then leads us and guides us into all truth. Romans 8:12–17 again shows us the power of the Spirit in us as a result of the grace we have received to live a life set apart to God:

> Therefore, brethren, we are debtors—not to the flesh, to live according to the flesh. For if you live according to the flesh you will die; but if by the Spirit you put to death the deeds of the body, you will live. For as many as are led by the Spirit of God, these are sons of God. For you did not receive the

spirit of bondage again to fear, but you received the Spirit of adoption by whom we cry out, "Abba, Father." The Spirit Himself bears witness with our spirit that we are children of God, and if children, then heirs—heirs of God and joint heirs with Christ, if indeed we suffer with Him, that we may also be glorified together.

When we are told not to *live according to the flesh*, this is not necessarily a reference to unclean living. It is speaking of a confidence in the flesh because of our performance. The apostle Paul says whoever does this will die. The law brings death. If we allow the Holy Spirit to empower us, we will deal with the appetites of the flesh and live. The law and works from the law can never deal with the flesh. Only the power of the Spirit working with the grace of God can change us from the inside out. We then have desires consistent with the grace of God in us. We are the sons and daughters of God who have not received the spirit of bondage to fear. This is a reference to the law. The law will always produce a fear of what is coming. This is condemnation.

We have instead received the Spirit of adoption, which is the Holy Spirit, the Spirit of grace who causes us to know our true spiritual lineage. Led by the Holy Spirit, we are children of God who no longer are under the dictates of rule keeping and performance. The Holy Spirit is working through the grace of God to empower us to live as those belonging to the Lord.

Transformed by Grace

One more Scripture I would like to point out is 2 Corinthians 3:15–18:

But even to this day, when Moses is read, a veil lies on their heart. Nevertheless when one turns to the Lord, the veil is taken away. Now the Lord is the Spirit; and where the Spirit of the Lord is, there is liberty. But we all, with unveiled face, beholding as in a mirror the glory of the Lord, are being transformed into the same image from glory to glory, just as by the Spirit of the Lord.

In speaking of the law, Paul said there was a veil over the eyes of those exposed to it. He said only in someone turning to the Lord and recognizing Jesus as Messiah is the veil removed. The law then begins to make sense.

If this turning to the Lord does not happen, all the law does is bring people into religious bondage. When they accept Jesus, however, the veil is removed and they come out from under the bondage of the law, into liberty. They no longer spend their time trying to keep the law and please God. The Spirit of the Lord lets them with unveiled faces be transformed into the image that the law could never bring them to. In other words, they come out of bondage and into the liberty of the Spirit of God. The grace they have received produces in them what they never could produce by just being religious.

The law only ridicules us for our failures to live up to God's standards. The grace of God transforms our heart through the Spirit of God. From the inside out, we begin to desire the desires of God. So we are saved by grace through faith.

Once this happens, this same grace works in us to fulfill the righteous requirements of the law. Not because we are performing or being rule keepers. We fulfill the passion of

God because we are now being empowered by the grace of God, through the Spirit of the Lord. We begin to produce righteous works because it is God's grace in us. We are new creations in Christ Jesus, prepared for good works. It is all a result of God's wonderful and marvelous grace!

FIVE

The Grease of God

Every one of us knows what it is to face difficulties. We probably know what it means to have traumatic experiences. We also are aware of being betrayed, hurt and wounded by others. This is part of being human. If we experience these things without the grace of God, they can make us skeptics and cynics who are pessimistic and bitter. With the grace of God, however, these places in our lives can be working something for us. This is quite an amazing thing—how something that seemingly is against us is actually working for us. Paul spoke of this in 2 Corinthians 4:16–18:

> Therefore we do not lose heart. Even though our outward man is perishing, yet the inward man is being renewed day by day. For our light affliction, which is but for a moment, is working for us a far more exceeding and eternal weight of glory, while we do not look at the things which are seen, but at the things which are not seen. For the things which are seen are temporary, but the things which are not seen are eternal.

Paul said he had found a secret to not fainting or losing heart. Even though things looked bad at times in the natural, he saw how that which was on the inside was getting stronger. Notice how he declared that what seemed to be working against them was actually working for them. It was allowing them to carry new levels of glory. He spoke of the *light affliction that was for the moment*. His ability to walk through these places by the grace of God allowed them to work for him rather than against him.

The word *affliction* in the Greek means "a pressure." It can speak of "a tribulation, a trouble or something that is stressful." The word *moment* means "an instance that flows by." These difficult places we walk through are meant to *flow by*. We are not meant to stay in them or be stuck there. If we get stuck in the effects of what is supposed to flow by, that place begins to fashion us. If we can find the grace in the midst of these places, this grace will fashion us rather than the difficulty shaping us. These places should be working for you a greater weight of glory.

If we can find that grace, we will move through a difficult situation and it will work for us. The whole issue is finding the grace in this place. Either the situation will fashion us for evil, or the grace available in the situation will work good in us and for us. This can apply to any circumstance we find ourselves in as believers. This word came to me when I was taking a nap on a plane while flying to minister at a church where the senior pastor just a month earlier had suddenly died. I had already been scheduled for these meetings long before the pastor's death, but when I heard what had happened, I was sure they would no longer want me to come. I figured the church would be in a very stressful place of transition. Yet they said they still wanted me to minister, which they felt could help them in this time.

I was not looking forward to the assignment. I felt completely unqualified to function in this situation. I had no idea what I would minister to a church processing through something like this. As I flew several hours toward this appointed time, I went to sleep and dreamed about the situation I was going into. I saw myself preaching this word about *flowing by*. I knew the Lord was saying to this people that as difficult as their loss was, there was a grace available for them. I knew the Lord was declaring that they had to flow through this with His grace. They could not allow themselves to get *stuck in the pain*. If they got stuck rather than flowing through it, they would miss the destiny God had arranged for them. He would empower them and bring them through this time with His grace. He would use it to qualify them to carry an even greater weight of glory/grace.

In 2 Corinthians 12:7–10, this is what Paul spoke of in his situation:

> And lest I should be exalted above measure by the abundance of the revelations, a thorn in the flesh was given to me, a messenger of Satan to buffet me, lest I be exalted above measure. Concerning this thing I pleaded with the Lord three times that it might depart from me. And He said to me, "My grace is sufficient for you, for My strength is made perfect in weakness." Therefore most gladly I will rather boast in my infirmities, that the power of Christ may rest upon me. Therefore I take pleasure in infirmities, in reproaches, in needs, in persecutions, in distresses, for Christ's sake. For when I am weak, then I am strong.

Paul cried to the Lord three times to deliver him. Instead, the Lord said, "My grace is sufficient for you, for My strength is made perfect in weakness." The Lord did not deliver him from this hardship, but instead gave him grace in the midst of it.

I have found that until deliverance comes, there is grace to strengthen us in difficult places. We do not have to traverse them in our own power. In fact, our sense of weakness in these places invites God to manifest His strength. We must not be afraid of our weakness. It is in our weakness that grace manifests. Paul actually said his thorn in the flesh was a *messenger of Satan*. This was allowed so Paul would not become prideful and arrogant because of the revelation he had received. Any arrogance and pride would pollute the truth God needed to pour through Paul. Some believe his thorn was sickness or something akin to it. I believe it was people who were persecuting Paul. Their badgering of the apostle caused him to reflect on and understand his own humanity. If we are true to biblical language, a thorn being against someone speaks of people, not sickness. Judges 2:2–3 shows God upbraiding the children of Israel because they did not fully obey him. It also shows biblically what a *thorn* is:

> And you shall make no covenant with the inhabitants of this land; you shall tear down their altars. But you have not obeyed My voice. Why have you done this? Therefore I also said, "I will not drive them out before you; but they shall be thorns in your side, and their gods shall be a snare to you."

Because the Israelites did not drive out the inhabitants as God had commanded, the inhabitants would be *thorns in their sides*. This idea is consistent in Scripture. Thorns speak of people and entities, not sickness, diseases or other problems, so I believe people who were driven by Satan were afflicting Paul. They were persecuting him and working against him. If you have ever had to deal with troubling people, you know the pain associated with this. It does have a humbling effect on you. God was allowing this to keep Paul where He needed him, so He could reveal even greater things to him.

In the midst of this, grace was Paul's only strength. In our places of hardship, when we cry to God we will either be delivered or find grace in the midst of what is happening. Paul found so much grace that he said he would actually take pleasure in these places of distress. In the midst of distress, we need to know that as we cry to the Lord, we should be looking for this grace.

Ephesians 5:15–16 tells us we are to grab the moment that has the power to alter our future: "See then that you walk circumspectly, not as fools but as wise, redeeming the time, because the days are evil." We are told to walk circumspectly, or with exactness. We are to walk in wisdom. In hard times, we should be measured in the steps we take and the decisions we make. Notice that as we do this, we are "redeeming the time." To *redeem* means "to buy up." We are to see this as an opportunity and not just as a hardship. There is something to be gained in this time.

The word *time* is the Greek word *kairos*. It means "an occasion." The idea is a moment. The other Greek word most prevalent for *time* is *chronos*. It means "a span of time." *Chronos* is what we live our life in. *Kairos* moments are the moments within *chronos* where the decisions we make alter the future. So Scripture is exhorting us to *buy up the moment*. Notice that this is happening in *evil days*. In every evil day or troublesome place there is a *kairos* moment, if we can see it and find it. We must not be so consumed with the evil occurring that we miss the moment where the future is altered into God's destiny for our life. When we buy up the moment, we will find grace in that place. Every *kairos* moment has grace attached to it. When we embrace the moment, we discover a grace we did not have before. We can come out of this stressful arena with another dimension of grace in our lives.

A grace-filled life is quite often a life walked through difficult and hard places. The grace the Lord grants in these difficult times can actually accumulate and saturate our lives with His graciousness. The hard, troublesome times of life when grace is discovered end up empowering us for our future. I am not who I am because of what I walked through. I am who I am because of the grace imparted to me in the process of what I walked through.

A grace can be on our lives that we would not otherwise have had without walking through these difficult ordeals. Just because we walk through hard places, however, does not automatically mean we gain new dimensions of grace in our lives. I have heard people preach that the difficulties of life mature us and perfect us. This is not necessarily true. They can make us bitter. If they are to fill us with grace instead, we have to respond properly. Hebrews 12:14–17 gives us some very valuable ideas concerning not missing the grace of God in these pressurized places:

> Pursue peace with all people, and holiness, without which no one will see the Lord: looking carefully lest anyone fall short of the grace of God; lest any root of bitterness springing up cause trouble, and by this many become defiled; lest there be any fornicator or profane person like Esau, who for one morsel of food sold his birthright. For you know that afterward, when he wanted to inherit the blessing, he was rejected, for he found no place for repentance, though he sought it diligently with tears.

The writer is exhorting us not to fall short of God's grace. In other words, do not miss the grace God is offering at a given time. It can have everything to do with whether we apprehend the future God has for us or not. The idea here is that grabbing the grace extended to us will empower us to live at peace with people and walk in holiness. We will have the right attitude and make the right choices because of a grace from God that is in our lives.

Falling short of God's grace creates an entirely different outcome. Notice that when we do not embrace the grace for our journey, a root of bitterness develops. This leads to immoral living and then produces in us the selling out of our convictions and values, which is what Esau did. We may then have allowed something for which there can be no remedy. All of this happens because we missed our moment of grace.

The Poison of Bitterness

Let's look more deeply at some of the things that can develop without grace at work in our lives. Bitterness is what occurs when we walk through hard places without grace. Without the grace of God, life's difficulties will turn us into that which we do not want to become. It is not that we just become a little upset and angry; the Bible actually declares that we allow a root of bitterness to develop. Bitterness is a poison. In Acts 8:23, when Peter addressed a man named Simon the Sorcerer who had become a convert, he spoke of this: "For I see that you are poisoned by bitterness and bound by iniquity." This is a root of bitterness.

In that our bitterness is caused by a root, it may be traced back to a certain event. In other words, an injustice or perceived injustice happened, and because we did not get what we thought was fair and just, anger developed in us that became bitterness. This ends up souring us on all of life, and we begin to see life through these lenses. We become convinced that everything is working against us. We begin to see everyone and everything as our enemy. This births a continual stream of anger and even fury.

Hebrews 12:15 says bitterness causes *trouble*. Things done out of bitterness will cause constant drama in our lives. The pot is continually stirred, so to speak. There is never peace for very long, because the anger in our hearts is right below the surface, ready to manifest at the slightest thing. The same verse also says this bitterness defiles many. Not only does it spew out and taint all within its reach, it also creates bitterness in others.

This is why Proverbs 22:24–25 tells us not to associate with an angry man: "Make no friendship with an angry man, and with a furious man do not go, lest you learn his ways and set a snare for your soul." Notice it does not tell us not to make friends with someone who is angry. It says an *angry man* and *a furious man*. This is not speaking of someone who is just having a momentary emotional upheaval. This is speaking of someone who is always angry and furious. The reason behind this is that there is a root of bitterness in that person. We are exhorted not to form a friendship or relationship with such a person. We are also told why. We are to avoid such people because they can influence us to the point of becoming like them. We will learn their ways, and a snare and trap can be set for our soul in the future.

Bitterness is a destructive thing. We must set our heart against it at all costs. It will destroy lives, relationships and futures. This all occurs because when an event happens, instead of finding the grace of God in that evil day, we fail to accept His grace. This is what Esau did, and it ultimately caused him to lose his rightful inheritance. It is so important for us to recognize and embrace God's grace in these times. Otherwise, this deathly process begins.

An Excuse for Immorality

Notice from Esau's example the next thing that can happen when we do not grab onto grace. We can become immoral people. When someone falls short of the grace of God and becomes bitter, the next step can be immorality, fornication and becoming profane. The bitterness in our lives will grant us license to fulfill the lust of the flesh. The sense of injustice we carry will tell us that we might as well indulge ourselves because none of our efforts work anyway. It will grant us the right we are looking for to do what our flesh is screaming to do anyway.

In Hebrews 12:16 the word *profane* in the Greek is *bibelos*. It means "a threshold," or "to cross the doorway." In other words, it says our bitterness will allow us to step into a place we never would have ventured into before. We will cross over a boundary and out of rebellion involve ourselves in lawless and destructive activities. Of course, this paves the way for lives destroyed and destinies demolished.

This scenario happens all the time. We often see it in marriages. When marriage partners allow injustice and anger to fester that lead to bitterness, quite often adulteries develop. Partners find themselves in places they never would have imagined before. As someone once said, "Adultery doesn't destroy marriage; it's the sign that it's already been destroyed." In other words, the bitterness and anger that caused and allowed for the activity of adultery are what ruined the marriage.

This all occurs because of conflict in the marriage that produced anger, and then bitterness. Paul actually addresses this in Colossians 3:19 when he says, "Husbands, love your wives and do not be bitter toward them." He presses husbands to love their wives with the God kind of love. This word *love* in the Greek is *agapao*, which speaks of the kind of love God loves us with. Loving this way is impossible for us outside the grace of God. Only by His grace can husbands love wives like this and wives love husbands. This kind of love causes us to deal with issues and not become bitter. Without this love operating in us and through us, we will not be able to be married without bitterness tainting or even destroying the relationship. There is a grace from the Lord that empowers us to love as we have been commanded. This grace will not allow bitterness to develop, and it safeguards our marriages and other relationships from ruin.

Selling Out to Bitterness

As the sequence of events continues because of falling short of grace, we can then move from becoming profane, immoral people to giving away and selling out our real purpose for living. Esau did this. He sold his birthright out of the bitterness of his soul, because of his lack of receiving God's grace. Genesis 25:29–34 shows Esau overstating his situation and selling his birthright to his brother, Jacob:

> Now Jacob cooked a stew; and Esau came in from the field, and he was weary. And Esau said to Jacob, "Please feed me

with that same red stew, for I am weary." Therefore his name was called Edom.

But Jacob said, "Sell me your birthright as of this day."

And Esau said, "Look, I am about to die; so what is this birthright to me?"

Then Jacob said, "Swear to me as of this day."

So he swore to him, and sold his birthright to Jacob. And Jacob gave Esau bread and stew of lentils; then he ate and drank, arose, and went his way. Thus Esau despised his birthright.

Esau was not about to die. Yes, he was hungry, but the bitterness he lived life with made him exaggerate his current circumstances. This allowed him to make the decision to sell Jacob his birthright. He made a transaction in the spirit world at this moment. When he swore that Jacob could have his birthright as the firstborn, he gave away that which was very precious. He was able to do this because of the bitterness in his heart, which allowed him to despise what should have been precious to him.

Bitterness we carry as a result of not living life from God's grace will cause us to make life-altering decisions that are not good. It will cause us to give away what is valuable. The truth is, the decision Esau made in this moment was irreversible. When he later wanted his birthright back, it was unavailable to him. It is said that he cried and wept over this decision later, but found no place of repentance. He was unable to recover from the decision made in that moment because of his bitterness of soul. All of this could have been averted, had he not failed to grab hold of the grace of God in his places of difficulty.

Making our decisions outside the grace of God can greatly disrupt the plan He has for us. It is imperative that we live our life in and from His grace. When we fail to grab onto that grace, our destiny and future become much less than what God intended.

Grace Is the Grease

To get a view of this grace that we are to find and live from in life's difficult moments, we should know that such grace is the grease to our lives. I grew up in a rural area and therefore learned to work on machinery and equipment. One of the things you learn early is that machinery must have grease and lubrication to operate properly for the long haul. Gears and moving parts will overheat and cause breakdowns if they are not kept lubricated with oil and grease. The oil and grease allow the moving parts to function without heating up, locking up and causing breakdowns.

Grace is like grease to our lives. It lubricates the *moving parts* of our lives and allows them to operate to capacity without internal problems arising. The moving parts of equipment and machinery that are greased are usually on the inside. This is where the grease is necessary. So it is with us. The grease of God, or His grace, is on the *inside*. It is within the inner man. This is what Paul spoke of in Ephesians 3:16, when he said he bowed his knees to the Father, "that He would grant you, according to the riches of His glory, to be strengthened with might through His Spirit in the inner man." This verse says it is the Spirit that brings strength to our inner man.

It is the Holy Spirit who ministers His grace into our lives, and we can then make our decisions from that place of peace He brings. In Revelation 1:4, "the seven Spirits" of God is a reference to the Holy Spirit and His different attributes and personalities, out of which He ministers grace and peace into our lives: "John, to the seven churches which are in Asia: Grace to you and peace from Him who is and who was and who is to come, and from the seven Spirits who are before His throne." When God's Spirit strengthens our inner man, it is because of the grace the Spirit is ministering into our lives.

The grace the Holy Spirit brings makes us strong and enables us to make the right and necessary decisions. He greases our life with the lubricant of grace that does not allow breakdowns. Esau's life was not greased with God's grace. The result was bitterness, which led to immorality, which led to a momentary decision to sell out, and which finally led to there being no way to recover—all because there was no grease of grace in Esau's life.

David spoke of God's lubricating grace in Psalm 23:5: "You prepare a table before me in the presence of my enemies; You anoint my head with oil; my cup runs over." As our Shepherd, the Lord *anoints our heads with oil*. This is what shepherds do for their sheep, primarily to keep the animals' wool from being infested with insects. These insects will swarm the sheep, get into their nostrils and nasal passages, and drive the sheep mad. Sheep have been known to beat their heads against trees and rocks, trying to remove the endless harassment of insects. They have also run off the edge of cliffs to their death, trying to get away from this torment. The purpose for anointing a sheep's head with oil is to keep this from happening. The anointing oil will not allow swarming insects to terrorize the animal.

So it is with us. The little torments of life cannot terrorize us when we are greased with the grace the Holy Spirit anoints us with. All the endless harassments are not allowed to work against us. What drives others mad will not land on us. The grease or lubricant of grace the Holy Spirit administers to our lives prohibits this. We will have no need to bang our heads against things in frustration or to run hysterically off cliffs to our demise. We are spared from this because of the grease of God's grace in and on our lives. We are lubricated because our Good Shepherd has cared for His sheep with His grace.

It is interesting that grace and peace are quite often mentioned together. In many of Paul's writings, he begins his greeting with grace and peace. First Corinthians 1:3 is just one of the many places where he uses this salutation: "Grace to you and peace from God our Father and the Lord Jesus Christ." Grace and peace go together, because wherever the grace/grease of God is in operation, there will be peace.

No matter what the circumstance might be, if we are lubricated with God's grease, the peace that Philippians 4:7 says surpasses all understanding will be on our lives. It will keep the bugs away. "And the peace of God, which surpasses all understanding, will guard your hearts and minds through Christ Jesus." This is an astounding Scripture. *The peace that surpasses all understanding* means it does not make sense in the natural, yet I have this undeniable peace. Many times when this is my experience, although things seem completely out of order I wonder if I am in denial. My natural mind would combat what I am sensing in my inner man. When it is the real peace of God, however, it is God testifying that everything is okay, no matter what it may appear in the natural realm. I have to choose to believe what I sense in the Spirit more than what I see in the natural. This is because grace and peace are coming to me from the Father, and from the Son, the Lord Jesus Christ, and from the Holy Spirit.

It is significant that this Scripture declares His peace will *guard* our hearts and minds. The word *guard* in the Greek is *phroureo*, meaning "to be a watcher in advance." In other words, the reason there is such a peace is because God is testifying that regardless of what it may look like presently, what is coming toward us is good. This is God releasing grace and peace to us. We can be confident in what we are sensing in the Spirit realm, even though the natural realm may presently be coming undone. The peace of God that is associated with grace is saying otherwise.

I have learned through the years to pay more attention to this peace than to what the circumstances seem to say. This keeps the little bugs and insects of the enemy at bay in my life. It allows me to live in the peace and grace of God during tumultuous times. When I do this, fear and uncertainty have no power over me. I can do what Jesus exhorted in Luke 21:18–19, taking possession of my innermost being and ruling over it because of the grace and peace I have received: "But not a hair of your head shall be lost. By your patience possess your souls."

The grace and peace of God that the Holy Spirit imparts to me brings confidence in His caring for me. I have the ability out of this to possess my soul. I do not let frantic emotions rule me. I rule over them because the grace of God in my life is keeping me greased and lubricated. When others are falling apart, I am standing because His grace empowers me to believe that not a hair of my head shall be lost. Through His grace, God is my strength and power. His grace is the grease to my life.

SIX

Grace Attached to Purpose

Every person who ever lived has had a desire to know why he or she was here. Every person who lives now desires the same. We all clamor to realize our purpose. This is because God has placed this desire in people's hearts. We are created with a divine design and an eternal reason for being. Paul speaks of this to his son in the faith, Timothy, telling him in 2 Timothy 1:9 that God "has saved us and called us with a holy calling, not according to our works, but according to His own purpose and grace which was given to us in Christ Jesus before time began."

Notice that our calling is not according to our works. In other words, God did not decide our purpose based on our performance. Wow! He decided our reason for existence and function in the earth according to *His own purpose and grace*. God created and formed us to fit into *His purpose*, based on what He needed us to accomplish. Our reason for being alive is because God needed us and made us for a God-ordained reason. Our purpose is connected to His historic agenda in the earth. Ephesians 1:9–10 speaks of this agenda:

> [God] having made known to us the mystery of His will, according to His good pleasure which He purposed in Himself, that in the dispensation of the fullness of the times He might gather together in one all things in Christ, both which are in heaven and which are on earth—in Him.

God purposed in Himself ultimately to gather everything back together that is in heaven and earth. When Adam and Eve fell, heaven and earth were separated. Through the work of Jesus on the cross, His resurrection and the coming of the Holy Spirit, heaven and earth are being reconnected. So whatever our purpose is in the earth is part of this greater and more splendid plan of God. We are here to be part of helping earth and heaven rejoin. We are here to help earth look again like heaven in its splendor and majesty. It is quite significant that Paul tells Timothy we were saved and called according to God's purpose and grace. Our reason for being here is to be part of the process of God reclaiming all things back to Himself.

Notice, however, that we also have been given grace. Purpose and grace were *given* to us before time began. Before there were the sun, moon and stars that began time, God arranged purpose and grace for us. This means that since before time started, something has been waiting on us to arrive and claim it. We are here to claim the purpose and grace that God appointed to us before we ever existed in the earth. We are not here to create something; we are here to discover something—our purpose from God, a purpose that has grace attached. The way we will know we are discovering our real, God-ordained purpose is because of the grace we will recognize in it. If it has no grace attached to it, then it is not our purpose. We were given both purpose and grace.

Purpose is what we are here to accomplish. Grace is the empowerment to fulfill it. We must not seek to fulfill something we have no grace for. To try to walk in something outside the grace of God for us will produce frustration, misery and death. Yet multitudes of people do this every day. They feel themselves sentenced to a life of no fulfillment and no satisfaction. Mick Jagger and the Rolling Stones sang the song "(I Can't Get No) Satisfaction." If you are familiar with the lyrics, you know they speak of the frustration of trying and trying, but ultimately coming up empty. The song speaks of falling for the world's marketing, which promises fulfillment if only this or that product is bought—only to buy it and find *no satisfaction*. It speaks of the emptiness of fame—the promise it offers, only in finality to discover *no satisfaction*. It speaks of romantic interludes that leave emptiness rather than enduring relationships. It tells of trying and trying, only to become weary and worn out, with *no satisfaction*.

This is the desperate plea of multitudes of people, and of generations looking for, but unable to find fulfillment. This is because they have not discovered the purpose of God that has grace joined to it. The real purpose of God for our life will always have a grace connected to it. This is one of the main ways we can recognize our purpose from the Lord. So many people struggle with what they are here to do. My admonition would be *look for the grace*. Wherever you find grace in your function, you will be looking at the purpose for which you were made.

This begs us to know what purpose with grace attached looks like. What are some signs that we are discovering the purpose we were made for because of the grace attached to it? There are at least five signs we can look for when identifying grace attached to our purpose. The first one is that we will enjoy what we are doing. The second sign is that we will be good at it. A third sign is that we will have success in doing it, and a fourth sign is that we can make money at it. A fifth sign is that in the process, the right people will favor us and see who we are. Let's look at each of these signs more closely so we can recognize them in the process of discovering our purpose.

Enjoying the Journey

When grace is operating in our lives, we will enjoy the function we have and its journey. That is the first sign that we are discovering our purpose. It will be a life-giving experience for us. Many people believe that whatever God has called them to will demand that they sacrifice their happiness. Nothing could be further from the truth. I would acknowledge that in some situations God may work in our hearts to desire what He wants, and it may be a process. In the end, however, when our life is yielded to Him, we will passionately desire what He wants.

Philippians 2:13 shows the working of God's grace in our life to transform our wants and desires to be consistent with His: "For it is God who works in you both to will and to do for His good pleasure." God actually is operating in our hearts and minds to cause us to choose His ways and to desire what makes Him happy. This began in us before time began and we existed in the earth. God ordained that we would exist, but before we were here in the natural, things were already in motion. Psalm 139:15–16 gives us amazing insight into our preexistence in the earthen realm:

> My frame was not hidden from You, when I was made in secret, and skillfully wrought in the lowest parts of the earth. Your eyes saw my substance, being yet unformed. And in Your book they all were written, the days fashioned for me, when as yet there were none of them.

The Bible declares that before I existed in the earth, there was a book written about me in heaven. Today, I am a reflection and depiction of what was written in that book before time began. I did not just show up in the earth. God planned me so carefully that He wrote the details of my life in His book before I was born.

I would like to examine this idea. When I have taught on it, I have usually referred to the book in heaven where each person is mentioned as *our book*. Technically, however, it would be more correct to say that it is *God's book*. I believe this is because it is filled with His purpose and agenda for our life, so His purpose in the earth can be accomplished. Again, this is about *Him*. We tend to try to make everything about ourselves. In reality, the main goal of all things is to get God's will done in the earth. We are told explicitly that if we will make this our main pursuit and not pursue our own stuff, our own stuff will be taken care of. Matthew 6:31–34 clearly speaks to this:

> Therefore do not worry, saying, "What shall we eat?" or "What shall we drink?" or "What shall we wear?" For after all these things the Gentiles seek. For your heavenly Father knows that you need all these things. But seek first the kingdom of God and His righteousness, and all these things shall

be added to you. Therefore do not worry about tomorrow, for tomorrow will worry about its own things. Sufficient for the day is its own trouble.

We are told not to worry. The key to leading a worry-free life is to make God's passion our own. We are to seek the Lord's rulership in every aspect of life. We are to give ourselves to what was written in *His* book concerning us. When we do this, all the things we contend with in life are taken care of. Our needs are met because we are meeting *His needs*. My destiny and purpose are written in God's book, and I get to be part of His purpose in the earth.

Notice also that what is in this book is what God *saw*. He *saw* me before I existed. God dreamed me up and fashioned me to *fit* into that which would be necessary. God would need someone to fill my place in His plan. As a result, He formed me to fill that position and place. I was formed for that purpose.

It would be helpful if we could think of the purpose of God in the earth as a big jigsaw puzzle He is putting together. Every one of us is a piece in the puzzle. As He was designing the puzzle in His mind, there was a hole where a certain piece was needed. To fill this hole, God designed you in His mind. He saw you individually and then wrote it down in His book concerning His desire and plan. He did the same for me. Every person's shape, form, personality, gifting and even disposition was planned for what He needed to fill a certain hole. This was all written down in His book.

This is also what *my substance yet unformed* means in Psalm 139. It is a reference to the intangibles in our life. The traits that make us interested in certain things and not interested in others were also written down. The characteristics

110

that make us unique were all noted in God's book. Science would probably call it our DNA. The genetic fingerprint of our uniqueness was determined before time began and was written there.

When I speak of this, I am speaking of the passions that drive our life—those strong impulses in us that we move toward and love. These are the longings of our hearts that begin to shape our activities and lifestyle. This is important, because this is what makes us gravitate toward what God needs us to do.

Because *my substance yet unformed* was predetermined, this means I will be drawn to what God needs and desires me to do. Just to be clear, however, I do not believe in predestination that makes us puppets on a string, with no real choice in what we do and become. I understand how that which was predetermined for me is always a *choice*, and I must choose to walk in it. God made a plan and purpose for me. I, however, must choose it. Yet I will have desires consistent with the purpose for me written in His book!

The thing that can interrupt this is *sin*. Romans 7:19 shows the apostle Paul struggling exasperatingly with this issue of desire. He declares, "For the good that I will to do, I do not do; but the evil I will not to do, that I practice." Paul desired to do the good, but he struggled against sin. Of course when we yield our hearts to Jesus, we then find His grace, which changes all of this. The grace of God will demote the desires of the flesh and will promote the longing of the Spirit for us conducive to what is in God's book. The more we surrender to the Lord, the more His grace accents the desires fashioned in our substance before time began. The result will be a longing in us for what God longs for in and through our lives.

We are also told that our days, *when as yet there were none of them*, were also written in God's book. This is a reference to how long we will live. I like this because it does not say years, weeks or months. It says *days*. God is interested in and even plans out our days. Again, I do not necessarily believe that we are puppets on a string, with everything we are to do every day mandated. We have choices. I do believe, however, that there are *days* critical to our divine purpose. What is to happen in these critical days can determine whether we fulfill completely what is written in our books. Choices made in these days have great impact one way or the other. We see this with the children of Israel. They had made choices all along the road of the wilderness. They had tempted and tested God and had not obeyed Him. Yet His plan for them was still intact. Even through their disobedience, God remained faithful to them.

This is what 2 Timothy 2:13 exposes to us: "If we are faithless, He remains faithful; He cannot deny Himself." When God makes a promise to us, He will keep His end of the agreement. He will not leave His part unfulfilled just because we are faithless. Yet there came a day in the lives of the nation of Israel when their rebellion on that specific day caused a generation to lose what God had for them. When God brought them to the edge of the Promised Land and they rebelled again and would not go in, this was a critical moment. In Numbers 14:22–23, we see that because of the children of Israel's unbelief, God decided in this moment to forbid this generation from going into the Promised Land:

> All these men who have seen My glory and the signs which I did in Egypt and in the wilderness, and have put Me to the test now these ten times, and have not heeded My voice,

they certainly shall not see the land of which I swore to their fathers, nor shall any of those who rejected Me see it.

All the other times of rebellion would have been overlooked, had they simply obeyed in this moment. In this *day*, however, they rejected the Lord and His word one too many times. The result was God forbidding any of them, other than Joshua and Caleb, from seeing and entering the land. This was a *day* made for them. What they did in this *day* would determine the next forty years of their lives. This was the *kairos* moment we spoke of before. It was a day when decisions had decades-long effects.

There were such days fashioned for us when there were yet none of them. We must be faithful to embrace these days when they are upon us. They can determine whether we fulfill the ultimate reason we are in the earth and fulfill God's plan for us. Because of what He wrote in His book about us, the Lord will call us to that which we have desires for. We can pay attention to our desires when we are submitted to Him, which will help us discern what it is He has for us to do. The grace we receive, given to us before time began, will cause our desires to be in agreement with God's will. I will therefore enjoy that which I have been graced to do!

Many times, the *leading* of the Holy Spirit is accomplished when we pay attention to our desires. We see this in Jesus' life when He would have compassion on people who needed healing and a miracle. At different places in Scripture, multitudes who were in need would surround Jesus. Yet at times, His desire toward a specific individual would be stirred. Matthew 20:34 shows Him feeling compassion toward two blind men. As a result, He released healing to them: "So Jesus had compassion and touched their eyes. And immediately their eyes received sight, and they followed Him."

The compassion Jesus felt resulted from His desire to heal these men. Jesus recognized what the Holy Spirit was leading Him to do because of the compassion He suddenly felt in His heart. Desire was the sign that He was meant to release the Father's grace in that moment. If we will surrender our hearts to the Lord, our desires will become clues to what His will is in us and through us. This is because whatever we are graced to do, our purpose, will birth connected desires in us.

Good at Our Gifting

A second sign that we are discovering our purpose with grace attached is that we are good at it. We will get more deeply into this later, but the grace we receive produces giftings in us. Romans 12:6 clearly defines how our gifts are a result of the grace we received: "Having then gifts differing according to the grace that is given to us, let us use them . . ."

Based on the grace given to us, we each have gifts different than other people. Grace determines the gifts we carry. This means whatever we are good at is because of the grace given to us before time began. Whatever our purpose is, our gifts will be involved. In other words, my gifts are joined to my divine purpose. If I want to know what I am in the earth for and am graced to do, I should examine my gifting and what I have a propensity for.

You may know what some of your gifting is. You may also not know what you are good at until you try it. Sometimes when people attempt something they have no idea they are gifted for, they not only discover a grace that allows them to enjoy it; they also find an ability to perform it well. This can happen in spiritual matters, but it also can happen in natural ones. For instance, whatever you have grace for, your mind will work that way. People tell me quite often that the way I teach and communicate spiritual principles makes them simple for others to grasp. The late Dr. C. Peter Wagner, one of my mentors and fathers in the faith, said to me, "You have some of the same gifts that I have. You can take complex things and make them simple."

I was astounded that a man of his regard would say such things about me. Yet he was right that my mind works this way. The moment I hear something or am shown a truth, my mind begins to break it down into simple ways to communicate it. This is not hard for me; it is just the way my mind works. Why? The answer is because I have a grace that causes my mind to work in this way, producing a gifting.

Quite often people who have grace that produces a gifting think that because something is easy for them, everyone can do it. This is not true. It is easy for them because there is a grace in their life for it. They are hardwired by God to think, act and respond a certain way as a result of the grace they have received. Also, because something is so natural and easy for them, they may not value it or realize what a gift they have from the Lord. We must realize that an ability we carry is because God has foreordained us to operate in this way. He granted us a grace before time began that is allowing us to function with ease in our gifted area. We must still recognize and value such a gift that comes easily to us, or it will not produce at the level it was meant to through us. We must take the gifting we have by grace and steward it wisely and faithfully. The gifting is a sign of the purpose we have been graced for.

Grace Brings Success

A third sign of our purpose with grace attached is that we have success doing it. Whatever grace we have received will bring us success. We will not labor and be fruitless. We will labor and see results. This is because we are not carrying out our purpose from our own strength, but from the strength and power of the Lord.

In my earlier years, I gave my life to many different efforts. I was able to contribute to some programs through my labors, but other things were very difficult for me. The position I was in caused people to expect certain things from me. For instance, when I was the pastor of a local church that Mary and I had raised up, people expected me to counsel them. After all, I was the *pastor*. This is what pastors do, right? The problem was, I really was not a pastor in my gifting. I held a pastor's position in that culture's eyes, but really, I was a prophetic apostle. This is my real gifting, which differed in some key ways from someone with a pastor gifting.

For instance, a pastor's main desire is to care for the people of God and see them healed and made whole on every level. This usually unfolds on an individual level as the pastor cares for the *ones*. The apostle, however, is usually more consumed with the *big picture*. Apostles desire to see the people of God reach their destiny corporately and have the impact on culture that the Church is to have. This is just one of the differences between a pastor and someone who functions apostolically. When I seek to explain these differences, I teach that all parts of the ministry/fivefold gifting should have a pastor's *heart*. Only a person graced by God as a pastor has a pastor's *gift*, however.

116

We all should care for people and their needs. Yet only the pastor, perhaps, has the gift to meet people's individual needs effectively as a shepherd. That was not my gifting, but because whoever leads a local church is typically considered the *pastor*, I was forced into a role I had no gifting to succeed at. This is the scenario many pastors are in today. Our culture *makes* whoever leads the local church a pastor, when in reality that person could be any of the five giftings mentioned in Scripture. The *pastor* might just be one of those positioned in the church under the leadership of the person God set in place to lead. Every church needs pastoral care, yet that may not be the gifting of the one who ultimately is leading the work. If we could conceptually get this, we would not have as much burnout in the ministry as we have today.

I was gifted to preach, proclaim, prophesy, heal the sick and perform other ministerial functions. I was not gifted to counsel. This was because I was not a pastor; I was an apostle by gifting, according to the grace I had received. I filled a pastor position, but I had no skill at counseling. I would sit for hours behind closed doors, listening to people's problems. Most of the issues were marriage issues. People wanted answers to these problems in their lives and home. It was literally drudgery and death for me to sit and listen. It was not that I did not care. I did care. It was that I just was not graced with a gift to do this kind of work.

I tell people now, "In all my years of counseling, I never saved a marriage. I almost lost one (my own), but I never saved anyone's." Why would this be? The reason is simple: I was not graced to do it. Therefore, I never had success in it. Trying to do what people expected me to do produced hardships and breakdowns. I no longer allow the expectations of people to push me outside my grace. Years later, I am now adamant that I only do what I am graced to do. I do believe there are moments when I can operate outside my grace/ anointing for a period of time. I do not, however, do this perpetually or ongoingly. To do so is to invite frustration at the least, and burnout and paralyzing discouragement that can lead to wrong choices at the worst. I now know that success is only the result of the grace of God at work in me and through me. If I am going to be fruitful and successful, it will be because it is grace in me.

The Richness of Grace

A fourth sign that we have found our purpose with grace attached is that we can make money doing it. Proverbs 10:22 tells us it is God's blessing that makes us rich: "The blessing of the LORD makes one rich, and He adds no sorrow with it." When we give ourselves to what we are graced to do, things begin to fall into place. Finances and prosperity can be part of that process. According to this Scripture, it is not hard work or even superior knowledge that produces riches. It is the *blessing* of the Lord. In other words, when His favor and grace are on us, our labors and efforts produce abundantly.

Notice also that the riches God's blessing produces are without sorrow. This seems contradictory to 1 Timothy 6:10: "For the love of money is a root of all kinds of evil, for which some have strayed from the faith in their greediness, and pierced themselves through with many sorrows." The love of money and desire for riches can produce many sorrows. Covetousness and greed are cruel taskmasters. The riches that come from the Lord's blessing and grace on us, however, are given for us to enjoy. When we are in the purpose of God for our lives and there is grace attached, the right people will favor us, and riches will be our portion.

Ecclesiastes 2:24 gives us insight into the blessing of God and the riches and prosperity it can produce: "Nothing is better for a man than that he should eat and drink, and that his soul should enjoy good in his labor. This also, I saw, was from the hand of God." To enjoy the labor of our hands and the prosperity in our lives is from the hand of God. It is a result of His grace to us. Ecclesiastes 5:18–20 gives us some further ideas concerning the blessings and grace of God on our lives and our prosperity:

> Here is what I have seen: It is good and fitting for one to eat and drink, and to enjoy the good of all his labor in which he toils under the sun all the days of his life which God gives him; for it is his heritage. As for every man to whom God has given riches and wealth, and given him power to eat of it, to receive his heritage and rejoice in his labor—this is the gift of God. For he will not dwell unduly on the days of his life, because God keeps him busy with the joy of his heart.

Notice that it is our heritage and a gift of God to produce and eat from whatever comes from His grace. The power to *eat* or enjoy something is from the Lord. I absolutely love the next part. It declares that we will not dwell unduly on the days of our life, because God keeps us busy with the joy of our heart. Wow! This is the grace of God in us and through us, bringing prosperity and life on every level. There will be no worries, no trauma and no drama. There will only be an expectant looking at the goodness of the Lord in our lives. We are *busy* with the joy of our heart. Grace attached to purpose produces finances and wealth.

Favored by Grace

The fifth sign of purpose with grace attached is that the right people will favor us and see who we are. In Galatians 2:9 Paul speaks of James, Peter and John helping him, and also helping Barnabas, because they perceived the grace on their lives: "And when James, Cephas, and John, who seemed to be pillars, perceived the grace that had been given to me, they gave me and Barnabas the right hand of fellowship, that we should go to the Gentiles and they to the circumcised."

It was the grace of God that these leaders perceived on Paul and Barnabas that caused them to give these two men the right hand of fellowship. In other words, they saw that God was with them because of the grace they witnessed on their lives. This allowed a platform from which to commend them to the purposes of God in the eyes of others. This helped Paul and Barnabas have a bigger, greater impact more quickly.

When the grace of God is on us, the right people we need to fulfill our purpose will give us their help and favor. Not everyone will favor us. We will always have our naysayers. But the right people we need who will help get us to the next levels of influence and impact will be granted to us. It will be the grace of God on our lives that will cause them to *like* us. They may not even know why they like us, but it will be because God's grace is pulling them toward us.

When this favor comes, we must know how to steward it. If we do not steward it properly, it can be lost. When the favor of God came on David in Saul's palace, he stewarded it with great wisdom. First Samuel 18:5 shows him using wisdom to do just that: "So David went out wherever Saul sent him, and behaved wisely. And Saul set him over the men of war, and he was accepted in the sight of all the people and also in the sight of Saul's servants." As a result of David stewarding this grace and favor on him, his influence continued to grow. The people liked him, and even Saul's servants were drawn to him. David stewarded the favor and grace on his life into great places of impact.

When grace is granted us, we must behave wisely. We must take that which has been given to us not as a license to act foolishly and arrogantly, but as a cause to serve humbly. David continued to honor Saul and go wherever he was sent. This allowed the grace of favor over David's life to continue enlarging.

When we steward favor rightly, it will enlarge continually. Luke 2:52 shows that even Jesus walked wisely in this way: "And Jesus increased in wisdom and stature, and in favor with God and men." The more favor we have as a result of the grace we are walking under, the more impact we can see. The result will be that the purposes of God are fulfilled in our life because of the grace apportioned to us. We will have the glorious privilege of being part of the historic plan of the God of the ages—all because we are learning to live in and function from the grace He has appointed to us.

SEVEN

Gifts and Grace

In the previous chapter, we spoke a little on how grace and the gifts we carry are connected. Gifts, by their very definition, are just that. They are not earned or won. They are given strictly out of the benevolence of our gracious Lord. Our responsibility toward the gifts we have is to steward them and be faithful with them. God entrusted them to us as a demonstration of His grace, and those gifts are meant to have impact. The more we can see how our gifts are expressions of His grace, the more we can appreciate them and be faithful with them.

We also talked about how the gifts we carry are a result of the grace we have received (see Romans 12:6). Notice that the gifts we have are determined by the kind of grace we have received. This means that grace is not just *one size fits all*. Grace has many different facets, and many different ideas attached to it. First Peter 4:10 shows us this concept with great clarity when it says, "As each one has received a gift, minister it to one another, as good stewards of the manifold grace of God." Peter exhorts each of us to minister out of the gift we received, as a good steward of this *manifold* grace of God. The reason there can be so many different gifts given to so many people separately is because God's grace is unique to individuals. Peter calls it the *manifold* grace of God.

Manifold in the Greek is the word *poikilos*. It means "to be motley or various in character." So the grace of God has many different shapes and colors to it. Because I grew up with an awareness of cars and how they operate, I know the term *manifold*. A car's intake manifold takes the fuel/air and dispenses them to multiple cylinders in the car. In other words, it starts with one source and multiplies into several outlets.

This concept of a manifold is exactly what the grace of God is. The one source is God Himself. Grace is the goodness and kindness of God toward us. This grace, however, has many different expressions as it is multiplied. In regard to gifts, the grace of God can produce all sorts of demonstrations. The gifts we have are dependent on the *kind* of grace we have received. Grace is the very nature of God at work toward us, and it can have varied displays and demonstrations. When we minister with these gifts to each other, there is a release of grace into people's lives. They begin to experience the very grace of God toward them.

The New Testament mentions basically three categories or lists of gifts that come from the grace of God. These lists are found in Romans 12:6–8, 1 Corinthians 12:1–11 and Ephesians 4:7–13. We will look at each list individually, in a chapter of its own, and see how the gifts we receive are intertwined with the grace of God in our lives. Let's start here with the first grouping, found in Romans 12:6–8:

Having then gifts differing according to the grace that is given to us, let us use them: if prophecy, let us prophesy in proportion to our faith; or ministry, let us use it in our ministering; he who teaches, in teaching; he who exhorts, in exhortation; he who gives, with liberality; he who leads, with diligence; he who shows mercy, with cheerfulness.

The word *gifts* in the Greek here is *charisma*. For those of us who are from the charismatic/Pentecostal ideology, this word is familiar. We usually think of *charisma* as being affiliated with being *Spirit-filled*. The real meaning of the word, however, is "deliverance, endowment and gratuity." It comes from the word *charizomai*, which means "to grant as a favor, in kindness, gratuitously, to pardon or rescue." The common understanding of this word is *gifts of grace*. We have gifts operating in our lives because they flow from the gracious character and nature of God. Again, we did not work for them, earn them or win them. We have these gifts because they flow out of God's graciousness toward His human race and toward creation. He ministers to these that He cares for so greatly from the gifts He entrusts to us as His people.

Many people believe that the gifts in this first list are those we were born with. They actually shape our personality and dictate the way we see life and respond to it. The grace involved in our formation would have been part of Psalm 139:16, our "substance, being yet unformed." God apportioned the grace that produced these gifts in us "before time began" (2 Timothy 1:9). Consequently, we were born with a certain kind of disposition based on the grace apportioned to us even before we were in our mother's womb. This was part of what was written in His book concerning us. We spend the rest of our lives discovering what was given to us before we ever existed in the earth.

Seven distinct *gifts of charisma* or *gifts of grace* are mentioned in this list from Romans. First is that of prophecy or a prophetic mentality. Second is ministry or service. Third is teaching, fourth is exhortation and fifth is giving. Sixth is leading or rulership, and seventh is mercy. Even though we can have a mixture of these ideas operating in us, one will tend to dominate our personality, disposition and the glasses we see life through. If we can understand this, we will stop trying to make everyone be the same. We are who we are, based on the grace of God given to us before time began. To try to reshape others into something not in their book will frustrate them and will not cooperate with the grace of God that is in them. They cannot help who they are in this regard. Instead of tolerating or even seeking to destroy who they really are, we should celebrate and honor them because of the grace God placed in them. Each of us, mixed together with each other, becomes a manifestation of the graciousness of God into the earth. None of us can accomplish this by ourselves. It can only be accomplished when we release each other into the grace God trusted us to function from.

The Prophetic Mindset

We each need to have an understanding of where we fit in, according to the grace of God we carry from before we were born. Let's take a look at these seven gifts individually and how they affect our life, actions, reactions and responses. The first gift mentioned is *prophecy*. Those who are driven primarily by a prophetic mindset will see things in black

126

and white. They will usually be people of justice and can become angered by injustice. They are focused on what is right and what is wrong. They also have a strong sense of what constitutes ethical and moral behavior.

John the Baptist is a biblical example of someone who carried a prophetic disposition. He called people to repentance. He saw things from the holiness and demands of the righteousness of God. Matthew 3:1–3 makes a powerful statement about John and what drove him:

> In those days John the Baptist came preaching in the wilderness of Judea, and saying, "Repent, for the kingdom of heaven is at hand!" For this is he who was spoken of by the prophet Isaiah, saying:
> "The voice of one crying in the wilderness: 'Prepare the way of the LORD; Make His paths straight.'"

Notice that John declared he was here to make the paths of the Lord straight. In other words, the way people perceived God had become warped. Who they thought God was, was incorrect. They had a twisted and perverted view of Him. John came prophetically declaring who the Lord really is. He called people to repent and line up with the correct idea of God, not the twisted idea of Him.

From the perspective of John's prophetic posture, there was no leeway—people had to repent and begin serving God correctly. John not only held this stance from his prophetic gifting, but also from his prophetic posture this charisma gift gave him. This gift was appointed to him before time began. He saw life through these prophetic eyes of right and wrong. It created in him a sense of the justice and righteousness God demanded. He lived, spoke and ministered from this.

Ready to Serve

The next gifting of grace is *ministry* or *service*. This word in Romans 12 in the Greek is *diakonia*. It means "an attendant in service or a waiter." It speaks of one who is waiting and watching to see what needs to be done and then to do it. People with this gifting see what others do not see. They then are quick to try to do the necessary practical thing. In Scripture, Martha is one of these. Luke 10:38–42 gives us insight into how someone with a gift of service operates:

> Now it happened as they went that He entered a certain village; and a certain woman named Martha welcomed Him into her house. And she had a sister called Mary, who also sat at Jesus' feet and heard His word. But Martha was distracted with much serving, and she approached Him and said, "Lord, do You not care that my sister has left me to serve alone? Therefore tell her to help me."
>
> And Jesus answered and said to her, "Martha, Martha, you are worried and troubled about many things. But one thing is needed, and Mary has chosen that good part, which will not be taken away from her."

This Scripture reveals several things about a servant. First, Martha *welcomed* Jesus into her house. People who are servants usually are given to hospitality. They love to serve others and make them feel welcome. They have a heightened sense of what makes people feel comfortable and uncomfortable. They will seek to create an atmosphere where people are at ease.

As with all seven of the giftings of grace, people with this gift have their positive sides and negative sides. This is why we need all seven gifts functioning in the Body of Christ to meet all the needs, but also to balance each other out. From her servant's heart, Martha became perturbed with Mary because she was not helping. This can be a fault of those who carry this gifting. They get upset with others and can develop a judgmental attitude when a job is not getting done. They can also have an attitude of "poor, pitiful me." This can happen because they do not recognize that others may not have the gifting of grace that they have. Servants have to guard their hearts against this and always *serve* the Lord with gladness.

Notice also that Martha wanted Jesus to tell Mary to help her. Servants sometimes actually complain to the Lord and want Him to deal with those who are not serving. Jesus' response was that at the time, Mary had chosen the good part, which was to sit at His feet and bask in His presence and life. This is what all of us should desire. Mary probably had this propensity because her gifting of grace was prophetic. That which she was gifted with drove her to desire the presence of the Lord rather than to serve, as Martha desired to do.

This is a good picture of how not understanding each other's giftings can result in conflict. Someone with a gift of service became upset with a prophetic person because she was not helping. Jesus said Mary had chosen the good part. We must free each other to be who we are. This does not mean we should not serve and help others. We should and we must. There are jobs that have to be done. Those with the gift of service, however, will delight themselves in these tasks. It actually scratches their itch, so to speak. This is who they are from the inside out. The Body of Christ needs this gifting of grace for service, or nothing practical gets done. When these people serve from their gifting, they are actually doing the most spiritual thing they can do. They are fulfilling who they are, because this is what is written in His book about them.

Delighting in the Details

The next gifting of grace Paul mentions is *teaching*. People with this gifting of grace love details. They are not content to know something works. They want to know *how* it works and *why* it works. The Greek word here is *didasko*. It does mean "to teach," but also "to learn." People who carry this gifting of grace are those who delight in learning. They love random information and facts. I have a friend whose father said about him, "Don't ask him what time it is; he'll tell you how to build a watch." This is a person who has the grace gift of teaching. These types may, in fact, even end up being teachers because they love information so much.

In America we have a game show called *Jeopardy*. I am always amazed at how much the contestants on this show know about a myriad of subjects. Many of these people carry this gifting of teaching. They love gathering facts and information. This can make them very successful on this show and in other ventures like it.

I think the apostle Paul carried the grace of teaching on his life. We know he was a teacher, but this is different from the gifting we are discussing of taking delight in knowledge. We will make this distinction more clearly when we look at some of the other lists of giftings found in the New Testament. Paul loved knowledge itself, and this flowed out of the grace of a teacher being on his life. This grace allowed him to be a breeding ground for the great revelation he would receive.

The fault or negative side attached to this gift can be pride. First Corinthians 8:1 clearly states that knowledge will produce pride if we are not careful and on guard: "Now concerning things offered to idols: We know that we all have knowledge. Knowledge puffs up, but love edifies." Paul battled the tendency toward being prideful because of the knowledge he had. Remember that even a messenger of Satan was allowed to harass him to keep him humble (see 2 Corinthians 12:7). This was not just because of his gifting as an apostle, but also because of his propensity to love knowledge. This flowed out of who he was by the grace of God.

From his innermost being, Paul loved knowledge. This allowed him to become an instructor to the ages. We are still gleaning today from the revelation he received two thousand years ago. This was allowed because of who God made Paul to be, by the charisma gifting He put in him before time began.

Calling People Near to Hear

Another gifting of grace is being an *exhorter*. This is an *encourager*. The word in the Greek is *parakaleo*. It means "to call near." The person with this gift is one who hates rejection and tries to make sure everyone is comforted and encouraged. Barnabas is definitely an example of this. Acts 4:36–37 actually says the apostles named him Barnabas instead of his given name for that very reason: "And Joses, who was also named Barnabas by the apostles (which is translated Son of Encouragement), a Levite of the country of Cyprus, having land, sold it, and brought the money and laid it at the apostles' feet."

Barnabas by nature was an encourager. Here we see him selling land and giving the money away. People with this gifting can be great givers. He was also one of the first to recognize Paul when others were rejecting him. Acts 9:26–28 shows Barnabas being used mightily as an encourager to open doors for Saul, who would later be known as Paul:

> And when Saul had come to Jerusalem, he tried to join the disciples; but they were all afraid of him, and did not believe that he was a disciple. But Barnabas took him and brought him to the apostles. And he declared to them how he had seen the Lord on the road, and that He had spoken to him, and how he had preached boldly at Damascus in the name of Jesus. So he was with them at Jerusalem, coming in and going out.

Through his testimony, Barnabas caused people who were rejecting Paul to be ready to accept him. This is what exhorters do. They will gravitate toward the underdog. As a result, they can help spare many lives that would otherwise be thrown away. This is who they are, by the grace of God.

The negative thing that can plague people with this gifting is taking up the offense of others. This happened to Barnabas. When Paul did not want Mark to go with him on a journey, Barnabas took up Mark's offense. Acts 15:37–40 shows Barnabas and Paul separating because Barnabas became offended:

> Now Barnabas was determined to take with them John called Mark. But Paul insisted that they should not take with them the one who had departed from them in Pamphylia, and had not gone with them to the work. Then the contention became so sharp that they parted from one another. And so

Barnabas took Mark and sailed to Cyprus; but Paul chose Silas and departed, being commended by the brethren to the grace of God.

Paul and Silas, the one Paul chose to replace Barnabas, were commended by the leaders. Barnabas, on the other hand, ended up in Cyprus with Mark. We do know that Mark and Paul were later restored (see 2 Timothy 4:11). There is some question, though, about whether Barnabas's ministry was as effective after his separation from Paul as it had been before that falling out. The point is that if we are encouragers, we must guard against offense—especially against taking offense on behalf of others.

Yet when we are exhorters by the grace of God, we can pick treasures out of what others might call trash. We will root for those people whom others place no value in. Many of them can become tremendous assets to the purposes of God in the earth.

The Grace to Give

The next gifting of grace is being a *giver*. There are people who are set in the Body of Christ to be givers. Of course, we are all responsible to give and to sow our finances. But there are those who have a grace on their lives to be benefactors for the Kingdom. We see some of these in Luke 8:1–3:

> Now it came to pass, afterward, that He went through every city and village, preaching and bringing the glad tidings of the kingdom of God. And the twelve were with Him, and certain women who had been healed of evil spirits and infirmities— Mary called Magdalene, out of whom had come seven demons, and Joanna the wife of Chuza, Herod's steward, and

Susanna, and many others who provided for Him from their substance.

Here we see that these women who are named, and many others (which probably means both men and women), ministered to Jesus, provided for Him and supported His ministry from their wealth. These were people who used their wealth and provision to advance Jesus and His ministry for the Kingdom of God.

People who have this grace on their lives love to empower the purposes of God with their giving. These are usually people who make lots of money, so they have the resources to do this. They are also people who like to make sure what they are giving is being used correctly. They see their giving as an investment to advance God's Kingdom. They also quite often are drawn to give to certain projects. Seeing things that need to be done can stir their hearts and cause them to have a passion to finance these projects.

The one thing these people must guard against is trying to control things with their finances. Even though they must believe in what they are giving to, they must not allow a controlling spirit to slip in. They must give what they give without being controlling, laying it down for the purposes of God. One of the main reasons these people have been empowered to accumulate wealth is so they can be givers and advance His Kingdom and His will.

Leading the Way

The next gifting of grace is *leading*. These are people who administrate and organize. They have the ability to arrange things and delegate people into places of responsibility. This gifting is so necessary if things are to be accomplished with a spirit of excellence. We can see this grace operating in Acts 6:1–7, when an organizational problem arose:

> Now in those days, when the number of the disciples was multiplying, there arose a complaint against the Hebrews by the Hellenists, because their widows were neglected in the daily distribution. Then the twelve summoned the multitude of the disciples and said, "It is not desirable that we should leave the word of God and serve tables. Therefore, brethren, seek out from among you seven men of good reputation, full of the Holy Spirit and wisdom, whom we may appoint over this business; but we will give ourselves continually to prayer and to the ministry of the word."
>
> And the saying pleased the whole multitude. And they chose Stephen, a man full of faith and the Holy Spirit, and Philip, Prochorus, Nicanor, Timon, Parmenas, and Nicolas, a proselyte from Antioch, whom they set before the apostles; and when they had prayed, they laid hands on them.
>
> Then the word of God spread, and the number of the disciples multiplied greatly in Jerusalem, and a great many of the priests were obedient to the faith.

The multiplication of disciples began to cause a problem. The Church was growing so quickly that it was outgrowing its organization. The solution was to set in place seven men who would oversee this issue of the widows' care. The dangers were that the problems at hand would stop the move of God, and that the apostles who knew their calling would be distracted from seeking His face. As those seven men moved with the grace of leadership, however, these dangers were avoided. Instead of what God was doing being stymied, it actually accelerated. This was because these gifted appointed men had leadership grace on them to oversee these matters. When leaders lead, organizational things are set in place and increase occurs.

One of the things those with this leadership gifting must guard against is becoming more task oriented than people oriented. If they are not careful, people under their leadership can begin to feel as if they are being used. Leaders must protect themselves from this tendency to focus mainly on the tasks and must always value people more highly than production.

Motivated to Mercy

The last charisma or gifting of grace mentioned in Romans 12:6–8 is *mercy*. God uses people whose motivational grace is mercy to demonstrate His kindness and compassion toward others. Mercy people will weep with those who weep. They have the capacity to feel the pain of those who are hurting. With the mercy gifting they carry, they have a unique ability to discern hurt in others. In 2 Timothy 1:16–18, Onesiphorus is said to have shown the apostle Paul great mercy:

> The Lord grant mercy to the household of Onesiphorus, for he often refreshed me, and was not ashamed of my chain; but when he arrived in Rome, he sought me out very zealously and found me. The Lord grant to him that he may find mercy from the Lord in that Day—and you know very well how many ways he ministered to me at Ephesus.

Notice Paul declaring that Onesiphorus and his house would find mercy because of the mercy they showed by refreshing Paul. They were not ashamed or afraid to be seen with him when he was thought to be a common criminal. This means they valued and loved Paul more than their own reputation. They did not wait for an opportunity to minister. The mercy gift in them drove them to seek Paul out. These were people who carried the gift of mercy and ministered it effectively.

Mercy people, however, must guard against getting sucked down with those who are hurting. If they are not careful, they can so identify with the hurt, pain and wounds of other people that they begin to take it all on themselves. This does no one any good. When I was a young minister in an associate pastor's role, I had a dream in which I was praying with someone who was trying to fall down. I was struggling to hold this person up even though the person seemed intent on falling down. I remember it being a real struggle to pray and physically try to hold up and stabilize someone at the same time. My pastor was also standing there with me. He was praying, but did not have his hands on the individual. I remember thinking, *Why isn't he helping me?* I then decided that if he would not help me, I would let the person fall. Sure enough, I let go and that is what happened. The person hit the floor. I then went over and sat down and began to sob into my hands.

My pastor came over in the dream and sat beside me and asked, "Robert, what's wrong?"

I responded, "All these people with so many problems."

He looked at me and said, "Don't take it so seriously."

I then suddenly realized that in ministering to people, I could not allow their trouble and problems to get on me. It was not my responsibility to hold them up. I was to pray, counsel and minister as best I could, but they had to choose to stand. This was a big revelation to me as a young minister. It set me free from allowing other people's problems to become my own. People with mercy gifts must guard themselves from taking on others' problems. Otherwise, they become good for no one. They become incapacitated and unable to love and minister effectively.

The Body of Christ needs those with mercy giftings tremendously. There are so many people with so much pain and hurt, and so many wounds. God will use those with this grace of a mercy gifting to pour oil and wine into the wounds of the hurting and help them get whole again.

Giving Place to the Grace

Each person carries a primary gifting out of these seven gifts of grace we have just discussed. We see life through our gifting and respond out of it. These gifts come with the grace God appointed to us before time began. When we can pinpoint which gifting is the primary gifting we carry, it helps us understand ourselves better. It can also help us know where we fit in.

Likewise, when we can recognize the primary grace gifting of others, it helps us relate to them. They may be seeing the same events of life that we see, but they see through different lenses. This is God-ordained. To contend with them when they are seeing things from a completely different perspective can be fruitless. If we all can only realize that those with different giftings are looking at life differently than we do, then maybe we can actually begin to value and treasure each other.

First Corinthians 11:29–30 tells us that we must *discern the body properly*. If we do not, negative things can occur:

138

"For he who eats and drinks in an unworthy manner eats and drinks judgment to himself, not discerning the Lord's body. For this reason many are weak and sick among you, and many sleep." In speaking of Communion or the Lord's Supper, Paul talks of eating and drinking in an unworthy manner. He says if we do such a thing, we can become weak, sick or even die prematurely. Such consequences mean we should take this seriously. While we see from this Scripture that *not discerning the Lord's body* is what causes us to eat and drink unworthily, we must also realize that there are two expressions of the Lord's body. There is the literal body of Christ that hung on the cross. His body is now in heaven, where He intercedes for us. Because of what Jesus did for us on the cross, we now have salvation, healing, deliverance and prosperity. His natural body, given for us, purchased all of this. When we properly discern what Jesus did in His body and by faith accept it, we reap the benefits associated with His sacrifice.

There is, however, a second expression of His Body—the many-membered Body called the Church. We must also discern this Body properly. First Corinthians 12:12 tells us that we are the many-membered Body of Christ and are therefore an expression of Him: "For as the body is one and has many members, but all the members of that one body, being many, are one body, so also is Christ." If we are an expression of who He is as Christ, we must properly discern this Body as well.

In other words, we must value, esteem and treasure who we are and our individual functions. This is where our understanding of the grace giftings is so essential. Otherwise, we develop judgments against each other because of the way we see things so differently. Offenses arise, and the things

Paul warned us about are enacted. We can eat and drink unworthily of the Lord's Supper/Communion and therefore become weak, sickly and even die prematurely. Instead of this sacred practice bringing life, it can produce death, all because we do not understand the grace of God in each of our lives.

May the Lord help us to discern His working in the Body of Christ. When we function as the many-membered Body of Christ in our giftings, we actually demonstrate God's heart in life's circumstances more effectively. Let's give place to the grace of God in others' lives, as well as in our own. When we do that, we cooperate and agree with the grace of God on people, and His purposes are accomplished.

EIGHT

The Supernatural Ability of Grace

A s I mentioned in chapter 7, we find three different lists of gifts of grace in the New Testament. We just looked at how each of us was given a particular grace gifting before time began (see 2 Timothy 1:9). We also saw how understanding the seven possible gifts mentioned in Romans 12:6–8 is essential to understanding ourselves and others. In this chapter, we will look at the next New Testament list, the nine gifts or manifestations of the Holy Spirit mentioned in 1 Corinthians 12:1–11:

> Now concerning spiritual gifts, brethren, I do not want you to be ignorant: You know that you were Gentiles, carried away to these dumb idols, however you were led. Therefore I make known to you that no one speaking by the Spirit of God calls Jesus accursed, and no one can say that Jesus is Lord except by the Holy Spirit.
>
> There are diversities of gifts, but the same Spirit. There are differences of ministries, but the same Lord. And there are diversities of activities, but it is the same God who works

all in all. But the manifestation of the Spirit is given to each one for the profit of all: for to one is given the word of wisdom through the Spirit, to another the word of knowledge through the same Spirit, to another faith by the same Spirit, to another gifts of healings by the same Spirit, to another the working of miracles, to another prophecy, to another discerning of spirits, to another different kinds of tongues, to another the interpretation of tongues. But one and the same Spirit works all these things, distributing to each one individually as He wills.

We normally call the gifts in this passage "the gifts of the Holy Spirit." Clearly, it is the Holy Spirit manifesting these abilities. This Scripture refers to these activities as a *diversity of gifts*, and the word *gifts* here is the same word we have spoken of before, the word *charisma*.

The Holy Spirit is the one who administers the grace of God that results in these gifts manifesting. The word *manifestation* mentioned in this Scripture is the Greek word *phanerosis*. It means "an exhibition, a bestowment, something apparent." It also means "a flashing forth." These gifts come out of the spirit realm and manifest in the natural realm. They flash from the spirit dimension into the natural, and they come from the unseen world into the seen. All of them are God's grace being administered into the lives of people in the natural realm, coming through the Person of the Holy Spirit.

These gifts/manifestations can be resident in a person's life, or they can be a temporary release of grace. For instance, someone can habitually function in the gift of prophecy because this gift is resident in him or her. The person who has this gift can, almost at will, discern things concerning other people. I know a functioning prophet who years ago would sit in parking lots and watch people coming out of the stores. He would seek to discern which car belonged to which person before anyone even got in. He was developing this gift of grace in his life, which he carries because it is resident in him.

On the other hand, this gift can come as a temporary release of grace. It can drop on someone who has never prophesied before, so that he or she prophesies with accuracy. This is sometimes called the spirit of prophecy, and it came on Saul before he was the first king of Israel. First Samuel 10:10–11 shows Saul encountering a group of prophets. As they prophesied, so did he. A temporary release of grace came on Saul because of the atmosphere he was in:

> When they came there to the hill, there was a group of prophets to meet him; then the Spirit of God came upon him, and he prophesied among them. And it happened, when all who knew him formerly saw that he indeed prophesied among the prophets, that the people said to one another, "What is this that has come upon the son of Kish? Is Saul also among the prophets?"

This temporary release can happen through the gifts/manifestations of the Holy Spirit as God releases His grace and goodness into people's lives. The truth is that in New Testament order, we can function in any and all of these nine gifts, as necessary. This is why the promise of the prophet Joel, quoted in Acts 2:16–18, is so powerful:

> But this is what was spoken by the prophet Joel:
>   "And it shall come to pass in the last days, says God, that
> I will pour out of My Spirit on all flesh; your sons and your

daughters shall prophesy, your young men shall see visions, your old men shall dream dreams. And on My menservants and on My maidservants I will pour out My Spirit in those days; and they shall prophesy."

As the Holy Spirit was poured out on the Day of Pentecost, Peter proclaimed that it was a fulfillment of this prophecy. The Holy Spirit would no longer just be for a small, special group of prophets, priests and kings. Now the Holy Spirit would be poured out on *all flesh*. Everyone would have the capacity to operate under the unction of the Holy Spirit.

At any given moment, those who belong to God and are His covenant people can be empowered to function in any of these nine gifts Paul mentions in the 1 Corinthians 12 list. The Holy Spirit can release the grace of God through a person filled with the Spirit of God. The Spirit can *flash forth* from the spirit realm into the natural with a supernatural exhibition of power and grace. Because of this, the person receiving the result of that gifting can be touched by God's grace!

A Passion for the Gifts

In 1 Corinthians 12:29–31, Paul also speaks of desiring the *best* gifts. The best gifts are the ones necessary for the moment, the ones that will minister the needed grace of God into a person's life. Paul asks, "Are all apostles? Are all prophets? Are all teachers? Are all workers of miracles? Do all have gifts of healings? Do all speak with tongues? Do all interpret? But earnestly desire the best gifts. And yet I show you a more excellent way."

We are told to "earnestly desire" the gifts that are best. This word *desire* means "to be zealous for, with passion and heat." We should, with great longing, want to function in these giftings. I think it is quite interesting that there has to be a passion for something before it manifests. In other words, only that which we are reaching for do we get. The Holy Spirit desires to release the grace of God into people's lives through these gifts. He needs vessels to do this through. We are those vessels, but we must be stirred with great passion to function in the best gifts. These are the gifts that will most effectively minister the grace of God to a person in a moment of time.

To effectively minister these gifts, we must realize we serve a living God. We just read 1 Corinthians 12:1–3, where Paul gives us three distinct guidelines for functioning in these gifts of grace. First, Paul declares that he does not want us to be ignorant concerning the things of the Spirit. Ignorance will cause us to miss the gifts of grace God wants to pour through us. We should learn as much as we can about these gifts. We should learn to recognize them and flow with them. We should learn to cooperate with the Spirit of God as He pours these gifts through us into humanity. We should ask the Holy Spirit to teach us His ways and show us how He does things.

The second thing Paul addresses is that we no longer serve dumb idols. This word *dumb* is the Greek word *aphonos*. It means "to be voiceless and mute." Paul is declaring that we no longer serve a god that cannot talk. We now have the *speaking* God. The nine gifts Paul is about to unveil are the ways God speaks and communicates through the Holy Spirit. His voice ministers grace to us through the Spirit's gifts. Luke 4:21–22 even says the same about Jesus' voice ministering grace: "And He began to say to them, 'Today this Scripture is fulfilled in your hearing.' So all bore witness to Him, and marveled at the gracious words which proceeded out of His mouth. And they said, 'Is this not Joseph's son?'"

The words that flowed from Jesus were *gracious* words. As Jesus spoke then, His words released grace. It is the same today. We are refreshed, empowered, strengthened and enlightened because of the grace of God being released from His voice. Our God is speaking today, and He does this through the giftings/manifestations of the Holy Spirit.

The third thing Paul declares is that the voice of God will always proclaim the Lordship of Jesus. The main purpose of the grace of God being released from these gifts is the further establishment of Jesus' Lordship in our lives. He has come to possess all His blood has bought. As the Holy Spirit ministers God's grace through these gifts, Jesus graciously takes more and more possession of us. He functionally becomes the Lord of our lives, until we are completely surrendered to His love and kindness in us. What a wonderful Savior we have. He is glorious and loves us into complete submission to Him. It is the encounter with His grace that melts us into absolute oneness with Him. We become totally His because of the effect of His grace on our hearts.

The Revelation Gifts

Let's look briefly at each of these nine gifts of the Holy Spirit that release grace into our lives. They can be broken up into three categories. The first category is the *revelation gifts*. These include the word of knowledge, the word of wisdom and discerning of spirits. The *word of knowledge* is when the Holy Spirit grants through supernatural revelation a piece of His vast knowledge. Just as a word is only a piece of a sentence, paragraph, chapter or book, a word of knowledge is only a small part of the overall knowledge of God. God knows all things. Hebrews 4:13 tells us that everything is unveiled before Him: "And there is no creature hidden from His sight, but all things are naked and open to the eyes of Him to whom we must give account."

Many times through a word of knowledge, God will let people know that He knows them, which brings them a great sense of His care for them. This can unlock deep places of ministry into people's lives because of the grace God is releasing to them through this gift. Proverbs 3:20 makes this statement about the power of God's knowledge at work: "By His knowledge the depths were broken up, and clouds drop down the dew." This can be speaking of the natural thing that occurs when there is rain, yet it is a spiritual principle as well. When God through a word of knowledge speaks into people's lives, it unlocks what has been held shut. Deep emotional and even spiritual bindings are released, all because God through this gift breaks open the depths of a person's heart.

The dropping of dew speaks of the gentle anointing of God that begins to flow because of this gift. Sometimes in these moments of grace, people's wounds are healed, bondages are broken, and even freedom from years of torment is set in place. A simple, yet profound word of knowledge unlocks the deepest places of a person's heart, and the grace that word carried brings him or her healing.

God will also use the word of knowledge to keep people from making terrible mistakes. When I was pastoring, I had a dream about a person in the church. In the dream, this person was planning on having an affair. I had actually officiated at the couple's wedding a few years before, and they were now well into their marriage. One Sunday, I noticed that the spouse from my dream was at the altar during a time of prayer, so I went over and whispered the content of my dream. Hearing it, the person immediately broke and began to weep, acknowledging that this was indeed what was going on. An affair was in the making, but the person repented and did not go through with it. The word of knowledge kept this spouse back from a sin that would have destroyed so much. God will use the word of knowledge graciously to help us make the right choices, even when we are going in the wrong direction.

A second revelation gift is the *word of wisdom*. Just as the word of knowledge is only a piece of God's knowledge, the word of wisdom is also only a piece of His wisdom. God has all wisdom. Colossians 2:3 tells us that in Jesus "are hidden all the treasures of wisdom and knowledge." When a word of wisdom is granted, it is a piece of that treasure being exposed. Wisdom is the understanding of how to apply knowledge. It is possible to know something, but not recognize what to do about it. Wisdom is an awareness of what to do. When God reveals a word of wisdom, He is showing us a secret of what to do about something.

Proverbs 15:2 tells us that the wise use knowledge rightly: "The tongue of the wise uses knowledge rightly, but the mouth of fools pours forth foolishness." Through a word of wisdom we gain an understanding of how to apply the knowledge we have. This results in problems being solved and breakthroughs coming.

I pastored for many years, and in those years I faced several times where a word of wisdom "saved" me in a situation. In one dilemma, there were two staff people who had held their positions for a number of years, and I saw no way for the church to reach its destiny and purpose with those two staying where they were. We had regular leadership meetings to deal with any issues facing the church, and as one particular meeting approached, I knew I was to ask for the resignation of both these staffers. I knew it was a word of wisdom and that this was the time I needed to do it. I was very concerned, however, because I tend to hate confrontation and I do not like to make people feel bad. Plus, I do not enjoy the tension and drama that confrontation sometimes can cause. Yet I saw no other way around this particular circumstance. I feared the Lord more than I disliked the discomfort that I knew my actions would most likely create. I knew this was a word of wisdom for this season of this church.

As we went into the meeting and began to deal with the necessary issues, these two staffers became angry and hostile toward each other. It got very heated and uncomfortable in the room. I knew this was my moment. I looked at both of them and said, "I want you both to step down from your positions."

One of the two reached into a coat pocket and pulled out an already prepared letter of resignation. This staffer had been planning on giving it to me and making a statement against my leadership anyway. Instead, I beat the person to the punch because of the word of wisdom, which drained the power out of that preplanned statement and letter of resignation. The other staffer also stepped down, and the church went on to the destiny God had planned for it. Even though I knew what needed to be done, I needed a word of wisdom on when and how to do it. With that granted, a huge explosion was averted and things came to divine order. This is the word of wisdom gift in operation.

The other revelation gift is the *discerning of spirits*. This gift can help us avoid being taken advantage of. Proverbs

7:6–7 warns us not to be simple: "I looked through my lattice, and saw among the simple, I perceived among the youths, a young man devoid of understanding." The simple are those who are able to be seduced and will believe whatever people tell them. I once worked with a middle-aged person who had joined us after serving in a poverty-stricken part of the world for many years. He was now ready to transition into another career, but was financially challenged because of all his years of service in such a difficult environment. Because I believe in honor and sowing for our own future, I felt led to pay off this person's debt and help him for an extended period of time in making his transition. He was going to accept this gift of help and over the next several years work toward getting things in place for a more secure financial future.

At first this man settled into the plan we had come up with, but then he began to get into some questionable investments. I had a dream that the people he was getting involved with were *burning* him. In my dream, he literally was burned! I knew God was saying that he should not be involved with the people behind these investments. I knew they were going to burn him by taking advantage of him. My dream was a discerning of spirits in this situation.

When I told the man this dream, he blew me off. He could not see that these people were taking advantage of him and stealing his finances, yet that is exactly what happened. As a result, his transition was greatly hindered and he was not able to move fully into the future he desired. God had wanted to make him aware through my dream of the truth of the situation and deliver him from the simplicity that was allowing him to believe the wrong things. Because he refused the grace extended to him, he lived to suffer the consequences.

God would have given him grace, had he received it from this manifestation of the Holy Spirit.

The Power Gifts

The second category of spiritual gifts that minister grace is the *power gifts*. The first one is the *gift of faith*. Faith is first because the other gifts of healings and miracles in this category require faith to function in them. According to Romans 12:3, we all have a measure of faith that has been given to us: "For I say, through the grace given to me, to everyone who is among you, not to think of himself more highly than he ought to think, but to think soberly, as God has dealt to each one a measure of faith." Notice that this measurement of faith determines the way we think about ourselves. Our identity is caused by this measure of faith. Anyone who has a self-image problem is not believing the right things about God and therefore about himself or herself. The bottom line is that we have been granted a measure of faith and we need to use it. Yet there is another dimension of faith, which is this *gift of faith*—the supernatural ability to believe God in a moment.

Whereas the measure of faith is something we are responsible to develop, the gift of faith is that which we are graced with in a given time. This allows the supernatural to occur. It allows us to step out in the moment and see God's hand manifest. This is what I believe happened to Peter in Matthew 14:28–31. Because of the word Jesus spoke to him, Peter had a supernatural ability to believe, so he stepped out on the water and did the impossible:

> And Peter answered Him and said, "Lord, if it is You, command me to come to You on the water."

So He said, "Come." And when Peter had come down out of the boat, he walked on the water to go to Jesus. But when he saw that the wind was boisterous, he was afraid; and beginning to sink he cried out, saying, "Lord, save me!"

And immediately Jesus stretched out His hand and caught him, and said to him, "O you of little faith, why did you doubt?"

Peter walked on water because of the faith that Jesus' words birthed in him in the moment. When the stormy conditions of the sea caused him to begin to question what he was doing, he then began to sink. Jesus saved him, but admonished him about staying in faith in these moments. This supernatural faith allowed Peter to step into a spiritual dimension to do the impossible. This is what this spiritual gift of faith we are graced with does. We see it happen in Acts 14:8–10, when Paul speaks a word as a lame man listens to him preach:

> And in Lystra a certain man without strength in his feet was sitting, a cripple from his mother's womb, who had never walked. This man heard Paul speaking. Paul, observing him intently and seeing that he had faith to be healed, said with a loud voice, "Stand up straight on your feet!" And he leaped and walked.

Paul recognized the gift of faith in this man at this moment, so he simply spoke the word and the miracle happened. In moments of faith, we must move immediately. The result will be a supernatural demonstration of God.

Another manifestation in the power gift category is the *gifts of healings*. Both *gifts* and *healings* are mentioned in the plural. It seems with this power gift some people have an anointing for certain ailments. It appears that they have greater success dealing with a particular kind of sickness. Acts 8:6–8 shows Philip having great success with the paralyzed and the lame:

> And the multitudes with one accord heeded the things spoken by Philip, hearing and seeing the miracles which he did. For unclean spirits, crying with a loud voice, came out of many who were possessed; and many who were paralyzed and lame were healed. And there was great joy in that city.

I am sure there were more than just paralyzed and lame people in Samaria. Others were probably also healed. It could be, though, that Philip had an unusual anointing for healing the group of people with this malady. He may have had a gift of healing for the paralyzed and lame. I have seen many people healed through the years of different kinds of diseases, but there is a significant anointing on my life for deafness. I have seen lots of deafness healed, and likewise loss of hearing and hearing impairment. Everything from a reduced ability to hear to total deafness has been healed. I consider myself to carry a gift of healing for deafness.

For instance, I was at a meeting in Ireland and there were some people present who had complete loss of hearing in at least one ear. One lady came forward who had lost her hearing in one ear as the result of a childhood injury. She had been thrown through the air in an accident and had landed on her head, resulting in a loss of hearing. As I simply prayed and put my finger in her ear, which had been closed literally for many decades, suddenly it opened. This was because of a gift of healing I carry to deal with deafness. I have seen this many times. It requires faith, but I also have a faith realm connected to the healing of this condition. With this faith realm to release the gift of healing for deafness comes an authority as well. The grace and goodness of God are manifested through His healing presence. Other people carry anointings for other diseases.

The other manifestation in the power gift category is the *working of miracles*. The word *miracle* is the Greek word *dunamis*, which means "a force." We get the word *dynamite* from it, so it is the idea of explosive power. In that it speaks of the *working* of miracles, there is the idea of moving in agreement with what God is doing. This is critical to the operation of this gift. Mark 16:20 declares that God was working with the disciples to back up His word with signs and wonders: "And they went out and preached everywhere, the Lord working with them and confirming the word through the accompanying signs. Amen." The word *working* here is the Greek word *sunergeo*, which means "to be a fellow worker." It is the word we get *synergy* from. Synergy is when two or more forces combine together to create a multiplied effect. So when the Lord *worked with them*, the result was signs and wonders occurring. They knew how to *work miracles*.

When we move in agreement with the Holy Spirit, miracles are the result. One time, a lady with a debilitating muscular disease came up on the platform. She had walkers in each hand, which were necessary for her to function. As she stood before me, I asked that these walkers be removed. Someone came forward and took them away.

Before I go on, understand that I am not suggesting you remove people's necessary medical devices when you pray for them. We are not doctors, and we believe doctors are greatly used of God. The instance with this lady, however, was a momentary effort of faith as I simply sought to move in agreement with the Holy Spirit. The lady was happy to do so as well. By God's grace through the Holy Spirit, we knew it was the moment for a miracle.

I prayed for this lady, without any real effect seeming to occur. By faith, I then took her arm and asked that she walk across the platform with me. As she struggled across it with me dragging her, suddenly the power of God came on her and went through her. She jerked away from me and began to run. She was instantly healed of her disease and was set free from years of torment. Her life and future were given back to her. This was the working of a miracle. We came into agreement with God and moved in faith until the grace of a miracle touched this woman's body. We worked with God, and God worked with us for the miracle of total healing to occur.

The Speaking Gifts

The third category is the *speaking gifts*. The first gift in this category is *prophecy*. Prophecy is not so much about *foretelling* as it is about *forthtelling*, or speaking *forth* the word of the Lord. This is why 1 Corinthians 14:3 speaks of edification, exhortation and comfort resulting from prophecy: "But he who prophesies speaks edification and exhortation and comfort to men."

Through prophecy, God releases His grace into people's lives. The word *edification* is the idea of "building up" and "confirming." Through prophetic utterance, people are confirmed in who they are. The fears that plague many are removed. People are set at ease and encouraged to move forward. The word *exhortation* means to "call near." It heals rejection and lets us know we are accepted by God. The word *comfort* means "to bring consolation." It heals the wounds of the past by declaring God's heart toward us. God uses prophecy to release His grace into the lives of believers and unbelievers alike. God uses prophecy to assure us of His love for us and of His undying heart to do us good.

The next speaking gift is the *gift of tongues*. My personal understanding of tongues is that it is prayer to God. First Corinthians 14:2 tells us clearly that tongues is speaking to God and not man: "For he who speaks in a tongue does not speak to men but to God, for no one understands him; however, in the spirit he speaks mysteries." If this is correct, it means that tongues is a prayer we offer to God by the Holy Spirit within us. When we pray in tongues in our own personal prayer life, we are talking to God, offering Him our intercession and prayers out of the ministry of the Holy Spirit.

We were in a prayer meeting one morning many years ago. I had a Haitian with us who had spoken the night before in our service. As we finished up the prayer time, this man came and asked me if I knew French. He spoke French because it is a prominent language in Haiti. I told him I did not. He then told me that every time I would finish praying in tongues, he heard me complete my prayer with *Je T'aime*. When he told me this, I realized he was right. He then told me it is translated "I love you" in the French language. Every time I finished my prayer, I was telling God, "I love You." I was astonished. I was not speaking to men as I prayed in tongues. I was speaking in what is assumed to be a romantic language, French, telling God how much I loved Him. This is amazing. Speaking in tongues is a powerful form of prayer where our spirit speaks to God even though our natural mind may be unfruitful. It is something we do by faith, out of the Spirit of the Lord releasing grace into and from our lives.

The last gift associated with the speaking gifts is the *interpretation of tongues*. This is where what is being spoken in tongues is understood. This is why 1 Corinthians 14:14–15 declares that Paul would pray and sing in the Spirit, but then also with his understanding:

> For if I pray in a tongue, my spirit prays, but my understanding is unfruitful. What is the conclusion then? I will pray with the spirit, and I will also pray with the understanding. I will sing with the spirit, and I will also sing with the understanding.

As Paul spoke with tongues in the Spirit, it caused his understanding to be open. He could then pray with his understanding in a known language with a greater depth. His ability to perceive the mysteries that he prayed about in the Spirit through tongues helped him receive revelation. I find this very empowering. One of my greatest ways of perceiving revelation is through praying in the Spirit and then beginning to receive understanding. This allows new ideas to begin to be brought into focus because of the mysteries being unveiled through tongues and interpretation.

These gifts we have just looked at, categorized into the three revelation gifts, the three power gifts and the three speaking gifts, are the nine gifts of the Holy Spirit we see in 1 Corinthians 12:1–11. God allows these charisma gifts to bring experiences of grace to people. He desires each of us to be His vessels, who can impart grace to others through what we have received.

NINE

The Gift of People

We have seen the seven gifts of grace apportioned to us before time began, and we have looked briefly at the Holy Spirit and His nine gifts of grace that can function in us and through us (see Romans 12:6–8; 1 Corinthians 12:1–11). In this chapter, we will look at how God, through His grace, makes *people* into gifts. They are not, then, just people with gifts; they are the gifts themselves. Ephesians 4:7–13 outlines five grace giftings in people that make them the gifts themselves:

> But to each one of us grace was given according to the measure of Christ's gift. Therefore He says: "When He ascended on high, He led captivity captive, and gave gifts to men."
>
> (Now this, "He ascended"—what does it mean but that He also first descended into the lower parts of the earth? He who descended is also the One who ascended far above all the heavens, that He might fill all things.)
>
> And He Himself gave some to be apostles, some prophets, some evangelists, and some pastors and teachers, for the

equipping of the saints for the work of ministry, for the edifying of the body of Christ, till we all come to the unity of the faith and of the knowledge of the Son of God, to a perfect man, to the measure of the stature of the fullness of Christ.

Here we see apostles, prophets, evangelists, pastors and teachers mentioned as people with grace giftings. The Greek word here for *gift* is *doma*. This is what the apostles, prophets, evangelists, pastors and teachers are. They are the people whom Jesus gave as gifts to His Church to bring it to maturity and to a complete demonstration of His fullness. When Jesus ascended into His heavenly place, Scripture says He then gave these *doma* gifts to the Church. Each of these categories has a special grace that makes the people within it who they are, for the benefit of the Church. Paul is clear about this in Galatians 2:7–9, where he says he is an apostle because of the grace he has received:

> But on the contrary, when they saw that the gospel for the uncircumcised had been committed to me, as the gospel for the circumcised was to Peter (for He who worked effectively in Peter for the apostleship to the circumcised also worked effectively in me toward the Gentiles), and when James, Cephas, and John, who seemed to be pillars, perceived the grace that had been given to me, they gave me and Barnabas the right hand of fellowship, that we should go to the Gentiles and they to the circumcised.

As we spoke of in chapter 6, Paul says it was the grace that Peter, James and John perceived in Barnabas and himself that made clear they were apostles. These leaders understood that the power to be apostles flowed from the kind of grace they had received. It was this supernatural empowerment that

160

caused them to function in this capacity. Whatever we are, we are by the grace of God. If we try to be something we are not graced to be, we will fail. If, however, we function in the gifts we are granted because of His grace, we will succeed.

Just as there are all sorts of corporations and organizations in the earth, the Church is God's corporation or organization. Through it He touches the world and advances His Kingdom. The fivefold ministry gifts of apostles, prophets, evangelists, pastors and teachers are five different functions/ offices that are necessary to make the Church successful and effective. These gifts of grace through men and women are primarily for the purpose of equipping and empowering the people of the Church. When these gifts function properly, the Church becomes an organism of power that changes the cultures of the earth.

The Individual Fivefold Giftings

I have also noticed that all people can be broken up into these five categories we see in the fivefold ministry gifts. It seems the grace that people with these five gifts carry—the grace that makes them who they are—can hold true for almost everyone, whether they are in the Church or not. Every organization/corporation that is successful, including the Church, will have people operating in each of these five functions. Let's take a look at these giftings individually, and you will see what I mean.

In the Church, the *apostle* is a general. Paul spoke of this in 2 Corinthians 10:4, when he said, "For the weapons of our warfare are not carnal but mighty in God for pulling down strongholds." The word *warfare* here is the Greek word *strata*. It means "a military service" or "apostolic career." It is what the word *strategy* comes from. Paul was declaring that as apostles, we are here to advance the Kingdom of God through strategy. He was declaring that every hindrance and blockage was being removed that resisted God's desire in the earth. This was the commission of apostles and an apostolic company. The thing that drives apostles forward is a passion to see the Kingdom advance. They are always taking new territory for their King, Jesus. In fact, one of the earliest uses of the term *apostle* was as a reference to an admiral commanding a fleet of ships. The mission of such apostles was to discover and take new ground for the king who sent them. They would conquer territory and establish colonies. This is what apostles do. This is the grace of God on their life.

Prophets are those who teach people to hear the voice of God. They do not just prophesy themselves; they teach other people principles that allow them to discern God's voice. The office and/or function of a *prophet* is given to the Church for this purpose. Just because someone prophesies, however, does not mean he or she holds the office of a prophet. Prophets who hold the office tend to operate in a governmental place in the Body of Christ, which allows them to shift things in the spirit realm and help give direction to God's Church.

Those who simply prophesy in the moment do not necessarily have this weight upon their function. Their prophetic abilities are for the purpose of exhortation, edification and comfort. This is what Paul declared in 1 Corinthians 14:3: "But he who prophesies speaks edification and exhortation and comfort to men." People are encouraged and empowered through this gift, which those holding the office of a prophet help nurture and release in the Church. This is why Paul told the Corinthians that everyone could and should *prophesy*, and it is why in 1 Corinthians 14:31 he gave them permission for all to prophesy one by one: "For you can all prophesy one by one, that all may learn and all may be encouraged." If all are prophesying, then it means all have been equipped to hear God. This is the primary job of prophets. It is to release a prophetic spirit that creates an atmosphere where people hear God and can then speak His word. The result will be that everyone is encouraged.

Evangelists are those who win souls and empower other people to do the same. Their passion is to see the lost saved. They have a unique ability to go wherever sinners are and see them converted. Philip was an evangelist who was mightily used of God. Acts 21:8 refers to him in this way: "On the next day we who were Paul's companions departed and came to Caesarea, and entered the house of Philip the evangelist, who was one of the seven, and stayed with him." This verse clearly depicts Philip operating and functioning in this office of the Church. We see also in Acts 8:5–6 where Philip conducted a great evangelistic crusade in Samaria and saw multitudes saved: "Then Philip went down to the city of Samaria and preached Christ to them. And the multitudes with one accord heeded the things spoken by Philip, hearing and seeing the miracles which he did." Notice that signs and wonders played a major part in what Philip did as a New Testament evangelist to convince multitudes to turn to Jesus. They listened to him because they heard and saw the miracles done through him. The result was a massive ingathering of souls for the Kingdom of God.

Pastors are those who care for the people of God. They shepherd them as the sheep of God's pasture, making sure they are fed, nourished and made healthy. In Matthew 9:36,

Jesus revealed His care for people through His desire for them to have shepherds: "But when He saw the multitudes, He was moved with compassion for them, because they were weary and scattered, like sheep having no shepherd." Notice that people become weary and scatter when there is no real pastor/shepherd gift among them. Pastors are absolutely necessary to the health and well-being of the people of God. They provide what miracles and other things never can.

The *teacher* is one who creates foundations and reveals truths that allow people to be established in their faith so they are not shaken. Teachers bring revelation forth that sets people free and allows them to become settled and secured in their faith. A teacher can take complex things and make them simple so people can embrace them. Paul is an example of someone operating in a teacher gifting. In 1 Timothy 2:7, we see him referring to himself as one of these teachers, as well as an apostle and preacher: "For which I was appointed a preacher and an apostle—I am speaking the truth in Christ and not lying—a teacher of the Gentiles in faith and truth." Only a gifted teacher could take the revelation of justification by faith and begin to unpack it. Paul's writings on spiritual matters have instructed people for millennia. His position as a fivefold ministry teacher continues to bring impact today.

Corporate World Giftings

This brief explanation of these grace giftings in people shows how God uses them to make His Church "corporation" successful. Yet these five categories are universal in any corporation that is having an impact. The terms for the giftings may be different, but the function of people operating in them is similar. For instance, in the business or corporate world there is an "apostle" who is called the CEO or chief executive officer. The corporate apostle is passionate about seeing the company's influence increase and expand. The grace you see on an apostle in the Church will similarly be on these people. They will be pressing things forward constantly to make their company more profitable.

Many times, entrepreneurs carry this same grace. It is who they are, by the grace of God. They are therefore able to birth businesses that grow to effective measures. This is because the apostolic grace is on them in the realm they function in. These apostolic people are especially capable at recovering something that is on the way down. Such was the case with Lee Iacocca and his tenure at Chrysler. Chrysler was on the verge of going out of business when they made the strategic move of bringing him in. Wikipedia relates this about Iacocca's time with Chrysler:

> Iacocca was strongly courted by the Chrysler Corporation, at a time when the company appeared to be on the verge of going out of business and had just sold its loss-making Chrysler Europe division to Peugeot in an effort to generate cash because the company was losing millions already in North America. . . . Iacocca joined Chrysler and began rebuilding the entire company from the ground up and bringing in many former associates from his former company.*

The result was that the Chrysler Corporation completely turned around and became solvent again. This occurred because a leader with apostolic DNA took the helm and directed the ship to safety and prosperity.

---

*Wikipedia, s.v. "Lee Iacocca," last modified February 27, 2019, https://en .wikipedia.org/wiki/Lee_Iacocca.

Every successful business/corporation also has something similar to the prophet. These are the visionaries and creative types. Creativity flows out of the prophetic realm. Whenever someone is creative, I recognize a prophetic grace on that person. These people think differently than others. They think outside the box and challenge us to new horizons. Any corporation must have these people, or times will pass it by and it will lose the market it has because others will see where things are heading and embrace change first. Without prophetic people of creativity in a company, what it once had will be lost. There must be the ability to sense the seasons and times and adjust. This is why creative/prophetic types must operate in any corporate setting.

For instance, the Swiss had a corner on the watchmaking market all the way into the 1970s. At that time, however, the quartz watch came on the scene. This was a watch that, among other things, did not need to be wound mechanically, but operated with a battery. The Swiss were hesitant about adopting the new quartz technology, because their mechanical watches almost completely dominated the market worldwide. They did not think a change was necessary, but they soon found their industry plunged into what later became known as the "quartz crisis." Wikipedia relates, "This period of time was marked by a lack of innovation in Switzerland at the same time that the watch-making industries of other nations were taking full advantage of emerging technologies. . . . This period of time completely upset the Swiss watch industry both economically and psychologically."* Within just two decades, employment fell in the Swiss watch-

*Wikipedia, s.v. "Quartz Crisis," last modified March 19, 2019, https://en.wikipedia.org/wiki/Quartz_crisis.

making industry from 90,000 to 28,000. The Swiss "quartz crisis" occurred because there were not prophetic people in this industry who could see where things were going. The result was the loss of an industry once dominated by the Swiss. Every corporation must have prophetic/creative people who can recognize where things are going and move ahead of the curve.

The evangelists in the corporate world are those in the sales department. These people know how to make products appealing. They have a sense of culture and the way it is presently thinking. They are able to present their product in such a way that it touches the culture so that people are willing to buy into what is being sold.

A prime example of this is Ray Kroc's influence on McDonald's. Kroc had an awareness of what people wanted and was able to deliver it. He moved restaurants into suburban areas and set high standards of cleanliness and even politeness to children. Wikipedia gives us insight into some of the strategies he used to build McDonald's into the corporation it has become worldwide:

> Kroc's policies for McDonald's included establishing locations only in suburban areas, not in downtowns since poor people might eat in them after the main business hours were over. Restaurants were to be kept properly sanitized at all times, and the staff must be clean, properly groomed and polite to children. The food was to be of a strictly fixed, standardized content and restaurants were not allowed to deviate from specifications in any way. There was to be no waste of anything. . . .*

*Wikipedia, s.v. "Ray Kroc," last modified April 2, 2019, https://en.wikipedia.org/wiki/Ray_Kroc.

These policies and others Kroc set came from an awareness of what would sell, and where it would sell. He had
an uncanny ability to perceive where culture was and give
it what it wanted. The result was the massive growth of a
corporation envied to this day.

The pastors in any corporate setting are in customer service. These are the people who not only take care of the customers' needs; they also make the customer feel important.
This means present customers stay committed and loyal,
while new customers are added. If a company loses customers because of poor customer service, it never advances. Customer service must be strong for an organization to enlarge
and advance in its purpose.

Take for instance the customer service commitment of
The Ritz-Carlton hotel chain:

> Ritz-Carlton's commitment to exceptional customer ser-
> vice is so strong that any employee is independently au-
> thorized to spend up to $2,000 per day to improve guest
> experience. That's right—whether an employee works at the
> reception desk, in the restaurant, or cleaning hotel rooms,
> they can independently decide to make a guest's experience
> exceptional. . . .
>
> In an interview with Forbes, The Ritz-Carlton Group
> President and COO, Herve Humler, describes the orga-
> nization's key to making customer service so stellar: em-
> ployee engagement. Humler noted, "I believe in the power
> of recognition and empowerment leading to great employee
> engagement. And employee engagement is critical to guest
> engagement."*

*Sophia Bernazzani, "6 Examples of Good Customer Service (and What You
Can Learn From Them)," *Hubspot* (blog), originally published September 26, 2018,
updated March 21, 2019, https://blog.hubspot.com/service/good-customer-service.

Herve Humler discovered a way to make people feel appreciated, important and significant. The result was return customers and customer loyalty because of unparalleled customer service.

The teachers in any corporate setting are those involved in providing continuing education. Things cannot be allowed to stagnate. People who work for the corporation must constantly be equipped for the next levels. They must be given the tools they need to do a better job. This is where the teachers/continuing education types come in. In his book *The 21 Irrefutable Laws of Leadership*, John Maxwell speaks of the "Law of the Lid." He explains that the skill and ability of those who labor with you determine how effective your corporation will be. Unless these key people are enlarged in their capacity to lead, motivate and empower, the corporation will hit a place of stagnation and limitation. At least part of the solution to this problem is continuing education where people are challenged, inspired, instructed and empowered. Such investment is necessary if those people are to play a part in the expansion of any organization.

When the apostle Paul spoke of these fivefold ministry giftings necessary to equip people to function in the Church, he was also revealing what is necessary to any successful organization. I believe that the whole population can be broken up into these five groups of people. It is important to recognize the grace that is on people to function in one of these five areas, and then to promote them into a place where they can do so.

If we could get people into their right place, they would flourish and bring great results to their corporate setting. The problem is that we have a lot of fish out of water. When people are functioning within their grace and gifting, they are happy and content. But most disgruntled employees are that way because they are not in their right environment and are therefore functioning outside the grace of God on them. The critical key is to recognize the grace gifting on a person's life and get him or her into a setting in agreement with it. When this occurs, success and impact follow.

In both Church and corporate settings, if people can be placed into their proper atmosphere and function, great advancement will occur. The truths contained in Scripture apply not only to the Church, but also to overall life. If we will see, understand and apply these principles we have talked about, whatever the setting, they will bring us the success we all desire. May we each discover the grace of God on our life and move in agreement with it.

TEN

Limitless Living

Discovering grace is the key to limitless living on every level. Things that have placed limits on us are removed when we understand grace and begin to live from it. Most people live with frustration because they are never able to live out their dreams. Living from grace causes things to shift and breakthrough into our dreams to occur. Jesus addresses this in Matthew 20:1–16, when He tells the parable of the workers in the vineyard and the landowner who hired them. This landowner had gone into the marketplace early one morning to hire laborers for his vineyard, agreeing to pay them a denarius a day. At the third hour of the workday, he went back and hired more laborers. Then he did the same at the sixth hour, the ninth hour, and even the eleventh hour, promising to pay each of these groups whatever was right. Notice what happened in verses 8–16, when it was time to settle accounts with his workers:

> So when evening had come, the owner of the vineyard said to his steward, "Call the laborers and give them their wages,

beginning with the last to the first." And when those came who were hired about the eleventh hour, they each received a denarius. But when the first came, they supposed that they would receive more; and they likewise received each a denarius. And when they had received it, they complained against the landowner, saying, "These last men have worked only one hour, and you made them equal to us who have borne the burden and the heat of the day." But he answered one of them and said, "Friend, I am doing you no wrong. Did you not agree with me for a denarius? Take what is yours and go your way. I wish to give to this last man the same as to you. Is it not lawful for me to do what I wish with my own things? Or is your eye evil because I am good?" So the last will be first, and the first last. For many are called, but few chosen.

Most people teaching on this parable will say that the point is that those who get *saved* right before the end will get the same reward as those who have served faithfully for a long time. This is not what I think this story is communicating. First of all, even though our salvation is of grace, our rewards are based on our works that come from the grace on us. Matthew 16:27 tells us that Jesus will reward us for our *works*: "For the Son of Man will come in the glory of His Father with His angels, and then He will reward each according to his works." We will be rewarded in God's eternal Kingdom for the works we have done as a result of the effect of grace on our heart.

The word *works* in this verse is *praxis*. It means "to practice and perform habitually," so it is speaking of a lifestyle developed as a result of grace changing and touching our heart. This is why the writer of Hebrews 12:28–29 admonishes us to serve out of the power of God's grace: "Therefore, since we are receiving a kingdom which cannot be shaken, let us have grace, by which we may serve God acceptably with reverence and godly fear. For our God is a consuming fire." Only by the empowerment of God's grace can we serve Him acceptably. Notice also that one of the reasons behind this is because "our God is a consuming fire." Everything we have done will be tested in the Day of Judgment. That testing will determine what rewards we do or do not get. Paul spoke of this in 1 Corinthians 3:10–15, showing that we must be careful what it is we build on the grace foundation we have received:

> According to the grace of God which was given to me, as a wise master builder I have laid the foundation, and another builds on it. But let each one take heed how he builds on it. For no other foundation can anyone lay than that which is laid, which is Jesus Christ. Now if anyone builds on this foundation with gold, silver, precious stones, wood, hay, straw, each one's work will become clear; for the Day will declare it, because it will be revealed by fire; and the fire will test each one's work, of what sort it is. If anyone's work which he has built on it endures, he will receive a reward. If anyone's work is burned, he will suffer loss; but he himself will be saved, yet so as through fire.

Paul is charging us as believers to make sure we build with that which is valuable, or live a lifestyle of good works. He says if we do this, we will receive a reward. If we do not build correctly from the grace he preaches about, we will be saved, but through fire. The fire of God's presence will burn up whatever we gave our life to. We will have eternal life, but no reward in it.

First Corinthians 15:10 exhorts us not to receive the grace of God in vain. Paul showed himself as an example of one who labored out of the grace he had received: "But by the grace of God I am what I am, and His grace toward me was not in vain; but I labored more abundantly than they all, yet not I, but the grace of God which was with me." If we are to receive a reward, we must labor from the grace of God. Paul declared it was God's grace working in and through him that caused him to work more than anyone. He was very careful not to boast in himself, but only in the grace of God.

Laboring under Law or Love

This parable of the vineyard laborers we started with is not about those who have no history with God getting the same reward as those who have faithfully served Him. It is about serving from works/law versus serving out of grace. Jesus is contrasting those who serve out of confidence in their own labors versus those who serve out of confidence in the goodness of God. All the groups mentioned in this story *worked*, yet it was the basis they worked from that was important. The basis they worked from determined the reward they got, rather than just their labors determining it.

Jesus pinpoints two groups in the story: those who *agreed* to work for a certain amount, and those who served on the basis of *whatever was right*. In the first group were the ones who had a *contract* with the landowner. Every other group *trusted* in his generosity, goodness and kindness. They chose to believe he would do what was right by them. In the natural, no one would take a job on the basis of *whatever is right*. We would want some assurance of what we would make before we started laboring. The fact that these laborers were willing to give their time without a guarantee of what they would receive speaks of the character of the one they worked for.

At the heart of this parable, Jesus is contrasting one basis on which people serve God with another, and the different results in their lives. The first group, who agreed to work under contract, represents the Jews, who served God under the agreement of the law. Jesus came to them first. In Matthew 10:5–6 He instructs the disciples to go out and preach only to those who are of Israel: "These twelve Jesus sent out and commanded them, saying: 'Do not go into the way of the Gentiles, and do not enter a city of the Samaritans. But go rather to the lost sheep of the house of Israel.'"

By mandate, Jesus had to give the Jewish people the first right to accept the New Covenant He was bringing. Only when they rejected it could He then turn to the Gentiles. This is why He initially refused the Gentile woman when she came seeking healing for her daughter in Matthew 15:23–24: "But He answered her not a word. And His disciples came and urged Him, saying, 'Send her away, for she cries out after us.' But He answered and said, 'I was not sent except to the lost sheep of the house of Israel.'"

God's intent was for the Jews to be saved so He could then use them to disciple and bring salvation to the world. When they rejected Jesus and who He was, however, God then decided to use the Gentiles to provoke the Jews to jealousy. We even find Paul following this procedure in Acts 13:45–46:

> But when the Jews saw the multitudes, they were filled with envy; and contradicting and blaspheming, they opposed the things spoken by Paul. Then Paul and Barnabas grew bold and said, "It was necessary that the word of God should be spoken to you first; but since you reject it, and judge

yourselves unworthy of everlasting life, behold, we turn to the Gentiles."

Once the Gospel was preached to the Jews and they rejected it, Paul said they could now, out of the protocol of heaven, take it to the Gentiles. This is what Jesus is ultimately referring to in this parable. Those who *agreed* and were the *first* group were like the law-following Jews. The word *agreed* is the Greek word *sumphoneo*. Among other things, it means "to stipulate by compact." In other words, they had a contract with the landowner. They had agreed to a denarius for a day's work. This was the common wage for a common laborer in those days. The contract the Jews had with God was the law. They understood that "if we do this, then God will do this for us." Their confidence was not in the goodness of God, but in their ability to keep the law and therefore be blessed. Jesus was seeking to bring them out of the era of the law and into the era of grace. He wanted them to stop trusting in their own efforts of righteousness, and trust instead in the goodness of God revealed through Him. This is the basis and message of this entire parable.

The problem is that legalism did not stop with the Jews. There are many *Christians* today who have also unwittingly opted to live legalistic lives of agreement with God, rather than trusting in His goodness. Galatians 3:10–11 expressly declares that if we choose to trust in our own efforts of works, we forfeit the blessing of faith in His goodness:

> For as many as are of the works of the law are under the curse; for it is written, "Cursed is everyone who does not continue in all things which are written in the book of the law, to do them." But that no one is justified by the law in the sight of God is evident, for "the just shall live by faith."

Through trusting in our own works and righteousness, we actually can place ourselves back under the curse Jesus delivered us from. Instead of living from the blessing of faith, we end up living diminished lives of less than the fullness of God. The sad fact is that if I seek to be justified by my own righteous activities, I then sentence myself to failure. There is no way I can keep all the law and be righteous. I will fail at some point. The Bible is clear in James 2:10–11 that if I am successful in keeping the law perfectly and only break it at one point, I am still guilty of breaking it all:

> For whoever shall keep the whole law, and yet stumble in one point, he is guilty of all. For He who said, "Do not commit adultery," also said, "Do not murder." Now if you do not commit adultery, but you do murder, you have become a transgressor of the law.

All that is necessary for me to be guilty is to break the law of God at one point. This means it is impossible for anyone to be justified by the law. We all need grace. The problem with the Jews was that they could not get it. They could not let go of the law and step into grace. This is also a problem for many *believers* today. We have many who trust in their own righteousness. As a result, they cut themselves off from the blessings of God because of the basis on which they are serving the Lord. They are laboring under the law, not love.

Taking It Personally

This became very real to me personally. I have been a man of prayer since 1980. When I surrendered to the ministry in my early twenties, I also understood that I was called to pray. I would set aside an hour a day of prayer. This was not "reading my Bible" time. This was time for praying and seeking God's face. During this time, I would usually pray for my family's financial needs. I did this for years. Over the course of time, I subtly began to think that I had to *list* my every need I wanted God to meet. This came as a result of reading a book by Dr. David Yonggi Cho titled *The Fourth Dimension*. In this book about how to pray in faith, Dr. Cho told a story about asking God for a bicycle early in his ministry so he could more effectively take care of his budding work.

No matter how Dr. Cho asked God for the bicycle, however, it never materialized. Finally, in frustration he asked God, *Why are You not giving me the bicycle?*

God responded, *Because you haven't told Me what kind of bicycle you want.*

Dr. Cho suddenly understood that he needed to be specific. He therefore told God the kind, color, size and style of bicycle he wanted. Within days, the bicycle was provided for him. Reading this story deeply impacted me. I knew I needed to be specific in what I asked God for, so I did what Robert Henderson tended to do back then. I took a valid spiritual principle and *turned* it into legalism. I began to tell God on a regular basis what my specific financial needs were. As they changed over the course of years, I changed my prayers. But always, in every prayer time, I would give God my specific list. I would tell Him I needed this much for the house payment, this much for the car payment, this much for my children's school and so on. I will never forget how, after years of seeing exactly what I asked for in prayer be provided, I went to prayer again one day and God stopped me. This time, as I began giving Him my list I heard Him say, *Stop agreeing with Me.*

The moment I heard those words, my mind went straight to the parable in Matthew 20 we have been discussing. By revelation, I understood that I was living like the first group in this parable. I was not trusting in the goodness, generosity and kindness of the Master of the vineyard. My confidence was in my *asking* God for the specifics, rather than having confidence in His kindness. At that moment, I repented and began to pray a different prayer that goes something like this:

Lord, I come before You. I no longer agree with You as a legalist. I repent for any and all confidence I have had in my own efforts. I can never be good enough or faithful enough to deserve Your favor. I trust Your goodness, kindness and generosity as the Master of the vineyard. I cease to agree with You legalistically, and now I trust You and Your grace to meet my needs and even my wants. Thank You for loving me and my family. My confidence is in You and in Your grace.

To my utter shock, the provision that began to come into our lives multiplied greatly. An exponential increase started immediately. When I stopped serving God by *agreeing* to the law and started trusting in His goodness, kindness and generosity by serving Him on the basis of *whatever is right*, everything shifted to a new level of blessing. Restrictions in the spirit world came off, and I was free to live in another place of grace. It was, and still is, amazing.

Some Secrets to Limitless Living

Let me show you from this vineyard-laborers parable what we can expect when we stop agreeing to some sort of legalistic contract and start trusting in God's goodness. This will uncover some secrets that will help us know how to live in and from grace. First, we must recognize that it is usually *not* what you do; it is *where* you do it from. In the parable, the hired laborers all *worked* in the vineyard. It was not about whether they worked or not. In fact, the landowner went out several times a day and *hired* laborers. We must recognize that when the Bible speaks against works, it is not suggesting that we put forth no effort. No! We must engage ourselves and move in faith. The issue is not putting forth effort. The issue is the basis from which we put forth that effort.

For instance, I did not stop praying after my revelation. I changed the *place* I prayed from in the spirit world. I stopped praying from the place of legalism and trusting in my own efforts, and I started praying from the place of grace and confidence in God's kindness and generosity. This changed everything. I was still engaged. I did not use this principle as a license for spiritual laziness. No, I understood that effort on my part was still required. But that did not make me a legalist; it made me a person of faith attaching to God's goodness through my efforts. This is where many people misunderstand the grace message. Grace does not relieve us from obedience. Grace empowers us to obey and even to work more diligently.

In what some have called the *hyper-grace* movement, this idea of grace empowering us to work more diligently would probably not be readily accepted. In this movement, people are taught that *nothing* is required from us. They are encouraged that God has done it all for us. In some of the more extreme hyper-grace teaching, people are even told that there is no longer a need for repentance after their initial salvation.

They are told that all their sins—past, present and future—are already forgiven.

I do not see this in Scripture. Neither do I see this in my personal journey with the Lord. Even though I do believe provision has been made for the forgiveness of all my sins, whether past, present or future, I also believe that I must, by faith, walk in repentance to get the benefit of this. It is not that I am trying to be righteous through my own efforts; it is that I am *responding* to God and His influence in my life through grace. My works become my own efforts toward righteousness only when I am seeking to create something out of my own strength and power. If, however, I am responding to the grace of God working in me, then my works are accepted and applauded by God.

The question becomes whether I am trying to produce something myself, or whether I am simply responding to God and His grace moving in me. The latter is what excites the Lord. I have found that when God desires to press me into new realms of holiness and righteousness, His Spirit of grace in me will convict me, deal with me and stir me toward this. I must, however, respond to this with efforts empowered by His grace. In these times, I will become aware if something I am doing or allowing is displeasing to Him. This can bring a troubling effect in my spirit and motivate me to repentance and change. When I respond in these places and times, I am moved into new places of consecration and holiness. This is produced not by works, but through responding to the grace my benevolent heavenly Father is granting me.

Another secret I learned to taking the limits off is that my reward is determined not by how hard I work, but by the desire of the vineyard's Master. Scripture says that when the first group in the parable complained, the landowner replied, "Take what is yours and go your way. I wish to give to this last man the same as to you" (Matthew 20:14). Notice that the reward of the one who only worked an hour was determined not by how long he worked, but by the desire of the landowner. Wow! We must recognize that when we, by revelation, put our confidence in God's goodness, His desire is stirred toward us. This moves God to bless us exponentially. This is why I saw an immediate increase when I changed *where* I prayed from in the spirit world. I was now placing my confidence in God's goodness, and His heart was stirred aggressively toward me as a result.

Another part of this secret is that we must reconcile ourselves to the fact that we can never earn what we receive. There is something in us that wants to feel like we *earned* what we get. The fact is, however, that I can never earn what God wants me to have. It is only a result of His goodness. If a day's wage was a denarius, those who worked only an hour did not *deserve* a denarius. They could never say they *deserved* it. They received it only because of the goodness, kindness and generosity of the landowner.

We have to decide this: Do we want what we can earn, or do we want what God's generosity grants us? I can place my confidence in my own efforts and they will produce for me, with limits. Or I can place my confidence in His kindness and it will produce for me, without limits. I have now learned to pray from this awareness:

Lord, I ask You not for what my labors produce, but I ask You even for that which I don't deserve. I am serving You from a place of trust in Your grace, kindness, goodness and generosity. I therefore believe You for exponential increase in my life that I could never earn.

The Multiplication Effect

An additional part of this secret of limitless living from grace is that my efforts will have multiplied effect. There were twelve hours in the vineyard's workday, so the laborers who worked only an hour received twelve times what those who worked all day got. This would mean that if the contracted wage was $10 per hour, those who worked all day would have made $120 for a day's work, while those who worked an hour also made $120.

This is amazing. If this was multiplied out over the course of a year at a given wage of $10 per hour, those who agreed by contract with the landowner would have made $37,440 per year for six twelve-hour days of work per week.

The given rate of those who worked based on the landowner's generosity, however, was $120 per hour. Remember, they had worked only one hour and were paid the same amount as those who had agreed to work all day. If these one-hour laborers had worked full-time at that rate, they would have made an annual salary of $449,280 for six twelve-hour days of work per week.

This can perhaps explain why some people work really hard and never get ahead. Maybe their confidence is in what their labors can produce, instead of being in God's goodness and generosity.

I challenge you, shift from a confidence in what you are able to produce to a confidence in what God's goodness can produce for you, and see what occurs. Maybe we will witness and experience the miracle of multiplication caused by the goodness and favor of the Lord.

A Lifetime of Favor

This next secret is one of my favorites from this vineyard parable. Out of this story, God spoke to me years ago about how He is looking for those He can bless so much that others will have a problem with it! This is why the landowner said to the complainers, "Is it not lawful for me to do what I wish with my own things? Or is your eye evil because I am good?" (Matthew 20:15). What a searching couple of questions, which the landowner uses to expose the evil in the hearts of those complaining. His first point is that everything belongs to him. He has the right to give it to whomever he wants, regardless of what anyone else thinks. This is why we should seek the favor of God first and foremost. The favor of people can be fleeting. Psalm 30:5 declares that the favor of the Lord is forever: "For His anger is but for a moment, his favor is for life; weeping may endure for a night, but joy comes in the morning."

God's favor being "for life" can mean it brings us life, which it does, or it can mean it is for a lifetime. I believe both are true. When we obtain the favor of God, which is a result of living in His grace, it produces what hard work never can. I have known many people who worked hard and yet never experienced the breakthroughs I am describing. I have known others who did not work nearly as hard and had a whole lot more breakthrough. This is because God's favor produces life for a lifetime!

The other part of the landowner's response is what intrigues me the most, when he said, "Or is your eye evil because I am good?" In other words, "Why are you having a problem with my goodness?" People have difficulty with the goodness of God, especially when other people are experiencing it. God is looking for people whom He can bless so much that it will expose the evil in others' hearts. What I mean by this is that there can be wrong perspectives about God that we all carry. Most, if not all, of us do not know how good God is. Through the landowner's generosity with those who had only worked a partial day, Jesus was showing us the Father's heart. At the same time, through the struggle of those who had diligently labored all day, He was unveiling the religious heart. Those laborers who had *agreed* to a certain wage were struggling with what was, in their estimation, the landowner's liberality toward others who did not *deserve* it. This event caused what was in these legalistic workers' hearts to be revealed and made manifest. Through the landowner's kindness toward those who had put their confidence only in his goodness came an epic revealing of God's heart toward people of grace.

God's goodness, His blessing of grace on people, exposes evil in the hearts of others. This is what we are part of as people of grace. God will bless those who leave legalism and step into grace so much that other people will have difficulty processing it. If we desire this to be our experience, we should step out of works and into grace. Then we will become the ones God will use to manifest evil, wrong perspectives in others about who He is. This is not our main intent since we are not trying to correct others by enjoying God's grace ourselves. We are simply walking in the goodness and kindness of the Lord. If He desires to deal with legalistic hearts because of His goodness toward us, however, that is His business. Our job in every situation is to love people. Yet in His wisdom, the Lord can and does at times use people like us to reveal new and different dimensions of Himself that others have missed or have misunderstood.

A Shift in the Divine

The last thing I will point out about living from this place of grace is that it brings a divine shift. Jesus finished the telling of this parable with a powerful statement: "So the last will be first, and the first last. For many are called, but few chosen" (Matthew 20:16). Sometimes we hear and think about this statement from different perspectives, but in this setting, Jesus is speaking it in regard to those who choose to live from grace versus those who live out of works and legalism. He is declaring, *If you choose grace and will trust in My goodness, kindness and generosity, then even though you are last, you will become first.*

Maybe you feel left out, abandoned, forgotten, used and even abused. The truth is, if you will shift in your heart and mind from being a works-oriented person to being a person of faith in God's grace and goodness, a divine shift can take place. You can move from being *last* to being *first*.

With a shift into grace, your times of unfulfilled dreams can come to an end. Your times of frustration at watching others be blessed while you feel left out can be over. You can see the limits imposed on your life come off, and you can begin to live a life without limits. This can occur because you have moved in the spirit world from works to grace.

From here on out, the sky is the limit. Step into God's grace and love and see the beauty of who He is shine forth over your life. New days are ahead!

ELEVEN

Moving in Grace

Learning to live from and operate in grace is a wonderful thing. We have seen how the grace of God can take the limits off our lives and move us into all we were made for. Exodus 33:12–17 shows us Moses crying out for the grace of God because he was aware of its power, and God agreeing to release it to him:

> Then Moses said to the LORD, " . . . Now therefore, I pray, if I have found grace in Your sight, show me now Your way, that I may know You and that I may find grace in Your sight. And consider that this nation is Your people."
>
> And He said, "My Presence will go with you, and I will give you rest."
>
> Then he said to Him, "If Your Presence does not go with us, do not bring us up from here. For how then will it be known that Your people and I have found grace in Your sight, except You go with us? So we shall be separate, Your people and I, from all the people who are upon the face of the earth."

So the LORD said to Moses, "I will also do this thing that you have spoken; for you have found grace in My sight, and I know you by name."

The first thing we should recognize is that *knowing* God is what produces the grace that He releases to us. There is no formula or gimmick connected to walking in grace. The grace of God in our lives is a result of intimacy as we get to know Him. This requires us to spend time with the Lord on an intimate level. Moses asked that he might *know* the Lord, that he might then have grace in His sight.

Knowing God is a result of revelation. Revelation is a result of intimacy with the Father. We can know about God, but actually *knowing* Him comes from our understanding being enlightened as we move into an intimacy with Him. This is why 1 Peter 1:13 tells us that grace comes to us as we receive revelation of who Jesus is. Revelation and grace are connected and joined: "Therefore gird up the loins of your mind, be sober, and rest your hope fully upon the grace that is to be brought to you at the revelation of Jesus Christ."

I realize that Peter is speaking of the Second Coming return of Jesus to the earth, yet the principle is still valid. The more revelation we have of who He is, the more we know Him and the more grace we walk in. Grace is something that should be increasing in our life. This is why we are admonished to *grow in grace* in 2 Peter 3:18: "But grow in the grace and knowledge of our Lord and Savior Jesus Christ. To Him be the glory both now and forever. Amen."

Notice that growing in grace and in the knowledge of Jesus is connected. The knowing of Him through revelation produces an increase of grace in our lives. We should ask the Holy Spirit to reveal new dimensions of the Lord Jesus to us. As these revelations take root in our life, new realms of grace will be imparted to us. Grace is always connected to who Jesus is! This is why John 1:17 tells us that "the law was given through Moses, but grace and truth came through Jesus Christ."

Different Levels of Grace

The very life of Jesus was and is a depiction of grace. When we receive Jesus, we get grace and truth. It is then our responsibility to continue growing in this grace until our very fabric and character reflect Him. The Bible mentions different levels of grace we can grow into. There is the level of *saving grace*. Again, Ephesians 2:8 tells us that our salvation is a result of grace obtained through faith: "For by grace you have been saved through faith, and that not of yourselves; it is the gift of God." What a wonderful truth. We are not saved because of our own works of righteousness, but because of His grace in our lives. Through this grace, His divine nature is imparted to us so that that which cannot die now lives in us. We are saved.

The next level of grace I see is *more grace*. James 4:5–6 tells us about this level of grace we can grow into: "Or do you think that the Scripture says in vain, 'The Spirit who dwells in us yearns jealously'? But He gives more grace. Therefore He says: 'God resists the proud, but gives grace to the humble.'" More grace comes to us as we humble ourselves before Him.

Notice that this Scripture speaks of the Holy Spirit in us yearning jealously. I take this to mean that the Holy Spirit in us is seeking to take possession of all that the blood of Jesus bought. Scripture is clear about how His blood bought us completely. First Corinthians 6:19–20 shows that the price Jesus paid for us means we are no longer our own; we were bought with the price of His blood: "Or do you not know that your body is the temple of the Holy Spirit who is in you, whom you have from God, and you are not your own? For you were bought at a price; therefore glorify God in your body and in your spirit, which are God's."

As a result of being bought at a price, we are now owned by the Lord. Even though He owns us, however, we have not yet fully been possessed by Him. This is one of the functions of the Holy Spirit. He is here to possess everything Jesus' blood has bought. This is a process. This is connected to *more grace*. As the Holy Spirit yearns jealously and works in us to possess us, more grace is released to us. Through the grace touching our lives, we are empowered to become more and more God's possession. This grace comes not when we resist this process, but when we in humility embrace it. In other words, grace comes when we surrender. When we cease our fight against the yearning of the Spirit and submit ourselves to God and His efforts to possess us, there is a grace we receive. When this occurs, instead of us giving up what we could never imagine letting go of, grace empowers us to yield ourselves completely. We functionally become not just owned by the Lord, but His possession.

Another level of grace Scripture mentions is *abounding grace*. Paul speaks of this level in 2 Corinthians 8:6–7, where he is addressing the church at Corinth about their financial giving: "So we urged Titus, that as he had begun, so he would also complete this grace in you as well. But as you abound in everything—in faith, in speech, in knowledge, in all diligence, and in your love for us—see that you abound in this grace also."

190

Notice that Paul sent Titus to *complete* the grace that had been started in them. He said something had begun in them that needed to be finished. In other words, they were not fully operating in a grace for giving the way they should have been. Notice also that Paul connected faith, speaking, knowledge, diligence and love all as results of grace. He commended this church for operating in grace in all these areas. The good things in the people were because of the grace of God operating among them. They needed, however, not only to have begun in this grace for giving, but also to be *abounding* in it.

Giving can be such a difficult thing for some people. They have attitudes about it and are even offended as a result of it. This is because they have never received the grace of God for it. Paul commissioned Titus to minister and develop this grace among the people. I am sure this meant Titus should teach on it and encourage them in it. When a grace for giving touches people, giving becomes a joy. There are several examples of this. Luke 8:1–3 shows some women whom Jesus touched, delivered and healed then giving extravagantly of their substance to Him:

> Now it came to pass, afterward, that He went through every city and village, preaching and bringing the glad tidings of the kingdom of God. And the twelve were with Him, and certain women who had been healed of evil spirits and infirmities—Mary called Magdalene, out of whom had come seven demons, and Joanna the wife of Chuza, Herod's steward, and Susanna, and many others who provided for Him from their substance.

These women had no problem giving abundantly and generously because they had been touched by His grace, which is the generosity of God. It is impossible not to become generous when you have been touched by His generosity. The women were abounding in this grace of generosity because they had been recipients of His goodness. When grace touches our life, it can take that which seems hard and make it life-giving.

This same abounding grace came on the early Church. Acts 4:33–37 shows people actually selling their land and inheritances and giving them to the Church and the purposes of the Kingdom. It also tells us *why* they did it:

> And with great power the apostles gave witness to the resurrection of the Lord Jesus. And great grace was upon them all. Nor was there anyone among them who lacked; for all who were possessors of lands or houses sold them, and brought the proceeds of the things that were sold, and laid them at the apostles' feet; and they distributed to each as anyone had need.
>
> And Joses, who was also named Barnabas by the apostles (which is translated Son of Encouragement), a Levite of the country of Cyprus, having land, sold it, and brought the money and laid it at the apostles' feet.

We are told that *great* or *abounding* grace was upon them all. This grace touching their lives was unlocking a liberality that most people would consider craziness. Who sells land and inheritances and gives them away to a ministry? Only those who have been touched by the graciousness and generosity of God. This grace unlocks His generosity in them. When this level of grace is unlocked over people, it brings them into a new realm of living. Second Corinthians 9:8 tells us the result of functioning in this abounding grace of God in giving: "And God is able to make all grace abound toward you, that you, always having all sufficiency in all things, may have an abundance for every good work."

The word *abound* here means "to superabound or be in excess." When this kind of God's grace is upon us, it takes us to a new level. It says we have a sufficiency in all things and an abundance for every good work. This means that all my needs and desires are met, plus I have abundance because of the grace of God I am now functioning under. Riches and prosperity are a result of the grace of God, or His generosity being unlocked in my life. He can trust me with wealth because He knows I will use it for the right reasons. The grace of God on my life will propel me to use it for His Kingdom purposes. As we step under this abounding grace, which Paul commissioned Titus to develop in the Corinthians, we will reap its benefits.

Accumulating Grace

Another principle to recognize about the grace Moses walked in is that grace accumulates in our lives as we obey. We saw that Moses declared, "If I have found grace in Your sight, show me now Your way, that I may know You and that I may find grace in Your sight" (Exodus 33:13). Moses was aware that grace could accumulate in and over his life. It was not only the result of *knowing* God through revelations, but also of walking in His *ways*. Moses was asking for more and more grace to come into his life. Of course, this is what James 4:6 declares as well, where we are promised more grace as we humbly walk before the Lord and in His ways: "But He gives more grace. Therefore He says: 'God resists the proud, but gives grace to the humble.'"

God resists the proud. The humble, however, are granted more grace. More grace comes as we obey the Lord and humble ourselves to take on His ways and not our own. The more we obey, the more grace empowers us, causes favor to come on us and increases our gift mix. Everything that grace does is increased as grace grows in and over our lives.

My pastor, the man who raised me up for ministry, eventually stood in my pulpit in the church Mary and I had birthed and raised up. It was a significant work, and as he stood before the hundreds of people in its multimillion-dollar complex, he was amazed. He spoke these words to the congregation: "I am shocked. I didn't think this boy [speaking of me] would make it."

Why would my pastor say this? Because in the natural, I did not have ability or talent. I was not gifted with strong spiritual gifts. There was nothing about me that said the Lord would be able to do such things with me. How did it happen? I discovered how to grow in grace. As I grew in it, the gifting that grace produces also grew in me. The favor of God increased over me. The graciousness of the Lord rested on me.

The more we walk in His ways and humbly serve Him, the more the grace of God increases. The result is that factors other people have not even recognized in us now produce success. God loves to take the foolish, empower them with His abundance of grace and confound the wise. Another lady from the church I was raised up in saw a post on Facebook concerning my ministry travels and activities. She actually commented in response, "Who would have thought it?"

In other words, there was nothing about me impressive enough for people to think I had that kind of future. There was no gifting or talent that testified about how God could use me in the nations. I was just a normal person with limited gifting. How did it all happen, then? I grew in grace and increased in the gifting God placed in my life. If you desire great impact, then let the grace of God bring enlargement to the gifts and favor you carry. Accumulate grace and grow in it. The result will be an increase in the level of everything grace creates and imparts.

Approved and Unique

Grace is also a sign of God's approval. In asking for grace, Moses said to God, "For how then will it be known that Your people and I have found grace in Your sight, except You go with us?" (Exodus 33:16). Moses was aware that it was essential for others to recognize God's presence over the Israelites as a people, and that such recognition would come because of God's grace on them becoming apparent. When people recognize the grace of God on you as a sign of His approval, it makes them a little less likely to assault you. When they know God is with you, they may not like you, but they probably will not attack you. Moses desired the stamp of God's approval, which was His grace, so that the people would be protected. In fact, this stamp of God's approval because of His grace will cause others to seek your favor. Instead of being your enemies, they will desire to become your friends—all because of the grace of God on your life, which produces success.

The grace of God Moses desired also causes us to be unique. As Moses petitioned God for this grace, he said, "So we shall be separate, Your people and I, from all the people who are upon the face of the earth" (also Exodus 33:16).

Moses knew that God's grace would cause this people to be different and unique. In today's world, people are all trying to be unique and stand out. This causes them to do outlandish things. They try to get the most unique piercings and tattoos, and they engage in all sorts of other unusual activities. People have a need to establish their own identity. Their pursuits are an effort to be separate from other people.

Moses understood that the thing that makes us unique is God's grace. His grace on our lives pulls out our uniqueness. It enhances our giftings with great influence. The uniqueness that everyone cries out for is realized through God's grace. As Moses cried out to God for grace, he knew it was that grace that would bring forth the Israelites' uniqueness.

The world is busy seeking to conform us. God is desiring through His grace, however, to make us stand out as His own special treasure. We were not born to fit in; we were born to stand out. Allow the grace of God to pull out of you that which makes you unique and different. Do not be afraid of it. Embrace it.

Praying from God's Grace

A final thought on the grace Moses sought from God is that it gets prayers answered. In response to Moses' request, God said, "I will also do this thing that you have spoken; for you have found grace in My sight, and I know you by name" (Exodus 33:17). God said He would answer the prayer of Moses because of the grace that was on his life. This is quite interesting. The key to answered prayer is that we pray out of grace.

We can pray without grace and maybe see no results, or we can pray from God's grace and see Him answer prayer.

Scripture actually speaks of this in Romans 8:26, when Paul writes that it is Spirit-empowered prayers that get results: "Likewise the Spirit also helps in our weaknesses. For we do not know what we should pray for as we ought, but the Spirit Himself makes intercession for us with groanings which cannot be uttered."

The Holy Spirit is the one who brings grace, empowering us in prayer. When we do not know how to pray because of our weakness, the Spirit comes and brings God's grace. These are the prayers that get answered.

It would seem that prayers laced with God's grace grab His attention. They have His aroma attached to them. As they come from our lives empowered by His grace, God is moved to answer them. May our prayers be filled with His grace and empowerment. Such prayers will indeed find a landing place in the very bosom of God.

TWELVE

The Finishing Touch of Grace

When I stand before the Lord, anything good I have done or have become will be because of His grace. The goodness of God that I received will have produced it all. Yes, I will have obeyed and cooperated. The impetus and driving force, however, will be His grace that has touched my life and overwhelmed me with His kindness and goodness. His grace will bring the finishing touches to my life.

The Bible actually speaks of this in Zechariah 4:6–9. Through an angelic visitation, the prophet Zechariah becomes aware of God's promise to Zerubbabel, whose responsibility it is to build the house of God and see it completed. The angel lets the prophet know that the whole process will be a result of God's grace. Zechariah is to declare to Zerubbabel that the Spirit of God will bring such grace into this situation that not only will he begin the work; he will also finish it:

> So he answered and said to me: "This is the word of the LORD to Zerubbabel: 'Not by might nor by power, but by My

Spirit,' says the LORD of hosts. 'Who are you, O great moun-
tain? Before Zerubbabel you shall become a plain! And he
shall bring forth the capstone with shouts of "Grace, grace
to it!"'"

Moreover the word of the LORD came to me, saying: "The
hands of Zerubbabel have laid the foundation of this temple;
his hands shall also finish it. Then you will know that the
LORD of hosts has sent Me to you."

It would not be a result of fleshly initiative. It would not be
a result of natural hype. This house would be wholly a result
of the grace of God supplied by the Holy Spirit. Zerubbabel
would move mountains and ultimately bring the capstone,
or finishing touches, to the Temple. He would do it crying,
"Grace, Grace to it!" In other words, the building of this
Temple would be a complete demonstration of the grace
of God.

So it is with our lives as God's temple. Scripture tells us
we are the temple of God both corporately and individually (see Ephesians 2:19–22; 1 Corinthians 6:19). Just as this
expression of God's Temple was built and completed in the
prophet's time as a result of grace, so shall our lives be. When
we stand before the Lord, we will see that in all the struggles
we have been through, in all the places we have walked, it was
God's grace bringing us through. We will know that our lives
are a depiction of His grace now and for the ages to come.
The grace that was developed in us through the adventures
and experiences of our lives will have formed us into His
image. We will be a living expression of Him, because of
His transforming grace.

This means we can have confidence that God will not
rest until He has completed all that concerns us. So often,

we can become afraid that we will not make it. We can be concerned that we are going to mess it up and that what God desired and intended will not occur. We must know that if we will simply yield and submit to the Lord, the same grace that began His work in us will also finish it. Several Scriptures speak to this. For instance, Hebrews 12:1–2 tells us that God not only authors our faith; He is also committed to finish it:

> Therefore we also, since we are surrounded by so great a cloud of witnesses, let us lay aside every weight, and the sin which so easily ensnares us, and let us run with endurance the race that is set before us, looking unto Jesus, the author and finisher of our faith, who for the joy that was set before Him endured the cross, despising the shame, and has sat down at the right hand of the throne of God.

We are told to lay aside anything and everything that would weigh us down in the race we are running. By the grace of God we let go of what would hinder us, so that we might run the race we have been given. We are assured that Jesus, who authored our faith, will also bring it to completion. We will not end up shipwrecked, but will reach the destination He has for us. He is faithful to do this. As we keep our eyes steadfast on Jesus and who He is, grace will be available to us to finish our course and win our race.

First Thessalonians 5:23–24 also tells us of His faithfulness: "Now may the God of peace Himself sanctify you completely; and may your whole spirit, soul, and body be preserved blameless at the coming of our Lord Jesus Christ. He who calls you is faithful, who also will do it." The Word of God promises us that God will sanctify us wholly and completely. He will keep and preserve us spirit, soul and body.

Notice that as the one who called us to this, He will also do it. We must move in agreement with Him, however. He is absolutely committed to our perfection. He will not abandon us in the midst of hardship or failure.

In fact, we are told that even when we are faithless, God will stay true to what He promises. The promise in 2 Timothy 2:13 is that even when we are weak and faithless, He will stay committed to His word and covenant, and He will not forsake us: "If we are faithless, He remains faithful; He cannot deny Himself." God does not take our moments of faithlessness as a reason to leave us. He cannot. Should He do this, He would deny Himself and not be a covenant-keeping God. If we in our failures turn and repent, God will remain faithful to us.

We also have His promise in Hebrews 13:5 that He will always be with us: "Let your conduct be without covetousness; be content with such things as you have. For He Himself has said, 'I will never leave you nor forsake you.'" The Lord is completely and unashamedly committed to us until all things are complete in us and through us. He even declares that when this reality touches us, the revelation of it will change our heart, desires and longings. The Lord Himself progressively will become the passion and pursuit of our life. His loving and gracious touch changes our nature to become like His. His being with us satisfies and fulfills every deep longing. His commitment to stay with us and never let us go touches the deepest need we might feel. Jesus being with us removes any fear of abandonment, neglect or rejection.

In a powerful and sure promise about our future, Philippians 1:6 declares that through the abundance of His grace, God will see to it that you and I are perfected, matured and completed, "being confident of this very thing, that He who has begun a good work in you will complete it until the day of Jesus Christ." This verse promises us that until the day Jesus returns to the earth, God will be completing the good work of His grace that He began in us. The Holy Spirit, imparting that grace to us, will continue to fashion us into God's image and likeness. This is so that when Christ appears we may be like Him, for we shall see Him as He is (see 1 John 3:2). Just as Zechariah prophetically promised that through the grace of God the Temple would not only be started, but also finished, so it is with us. The Lord will perfect what concerns us. He will not give up and leave us. We are and will be a product of His grace.

Crossing the Finish Line

I was in a service in South Dakota one Sunday when the pastor, who also functioned as the worship leader, began to sing a *prophetic song*. In other words, it was not a song written on paper, but one flowing spontaneously out of his heart and spirit. He began to sing as if the heavenlies and those residing there were singing over us as a congregation, "You're going to make it! You're going to cross the finish line!"

As the pastor/the heavenlies sang this several times, the awesome presence and grace of God filled the sanctuary. People were weeping as the fears they carried of not being good enough or faithful enough or strong enough began to vanish in the midst of an expression of God's grace. The Lord used this song of confidence and assurance to birth in us that day an awareness that what He had started, He was committed to finishing. We were going to make it! We were going to cross the finish line!

God was not saying this necessarily because He had such great confidence in us. He was saying it because of His confidence in His grace in us. What God has started, He will finish. I have often wondered why God asked Satan in Job 1:8–9 whether he had considered Job. I think God posed this question knowing that Satan would challenge it, yet also knowing that the grace on Job would win out:

> Then the LORD said to Satan, "Have you considered My servant Job, that there is none like him on the earth, a blameless and upright man, one who fears God and shuns evil?"
>
> So Satan answered the LORD and said, "Does Job fear God for nothing?"

If you were to read the rest of this discourse, you would discover that the result of God's question was Job's whole life being thrown into massive trouble and tribulation. I have often wondered why God would initiate such a thing. I believe it was because God wanted to work some things into His faithful servant Job, as well as work some things out of him. God was not afraid that Job would forsake Him in the process. I believe God's confidence was in His grace that was on Job. God had absolute confidence in His grace being able to keep Job, hold Job and sustain Job through this entire place. The Lord was more confident in His grace on Job than He was afraid that Satan would overwhelm and detour His servant.

The Lord is not in panic mode about us either. He is full of boldness and assurance about us making it. He knows the finishing touches of our life will come as a result of His powerful and sufficient grace.

Grace for the Journey

One more thing I would mention about grace. It is the means by which we will transition from this life into the next. Hebrews 2:9 tells us that what Jesus did for us through dying, He did in the power of God's grace: "But we see Jesus, who was made a little lower than the angels, for the suffering of death crowned with glory and honor, that He, by the grace of God, might taste death for everyone."

Even Jesus walked through the place of death by the grace of God. This tells me that as any of us approach our time of departure from this life into the next, there will be grace for that journey. God will grant us the grace to make that transition into the life to come. This is of great assurance. There are so many unknowns concerning this particular juncture in our life. It is of great comfort that those who belong to God will have the grace to make it, just as Jesus did. If Jesus needed grace for this time, how much more do we?

In the story Jesus told in Luke 16:19–31 of the beggar and the rich man who both died, the beggar had an angelic escort to his place in the afterlife: "So it was that the beggar died, and was carried by the angels to Abraham's bosom. The rich man also died and was buried" (verse 22). This beggar had grace for the transition that involved angels carrying him to his destination. When we come to this place in our lives, the same grace that began God's work in us will continue. We will not be left to navigate it on our own. The same grace we were granted that empowered us to grasp the salvation offered us will be there. The grace that empowered us with our abilities that we used to bless and minister in this life will be there. The grace that walked with us through every storm and difficulty will be there. The grace that will continue through the ages to come, manifesting God's kindness to us, will be there. The grace supplied by the Holy Spirit, who started the good work in us, will also finish it.

Galatians 3:2–3 encourages us that the same Holy Spirit who brought God's grace to us will be the one who will see us through to the end: "This only I want to learn from you: Did you receive the Spirit by the works of the law, or by the hearing of faith? Are you so foolish? Having begun in the Spirit, are you now being made perfect by the flesh?" The Lord will not change the game plan. We will not be made perfect through our own efforts toward righteousness. It will be the grace of God the Spirit brought us that will complete the work in us. We must not revert to attempting to be righteous out of our own efforts.

Only as we continually allow the grace of God to work in us and produce in us His character and nature will we mature. He will bring us into the expression of who He is. It will be the power of His grace made manifest in us. All of eternity will proclaim with Ephesians 1:6 that everything in us was done "to the praise of the glory of His grace, by which He made us accepted in the Beloved" (Ephesians 1:6).

God's grace that began the work will complete it. For all of eternity, we will stand amazed at His grace. We will delight ourselves in the splendor and glory of His marvelous grace. He will bring the finishing touches to our lives. We will cry, *"Grace, grace to it!"* as we marvel at the unsearchable kindness of who He is.

Robert Henderson is an apostolic leader driven by a mandate to disciple the nations through writing and speaking. He travels extensively around the globe to teach the truths of Scripture with both simplicity and clarity. Operating in revelation and impartation, he then empowers the Body of Christ to apply these scriptural truths to find breakthrough in many vital areas.

Robert's teachings focus on the apostolic, the Kingdom of God, the Seven Mountains and, most notably, the "Courts of Heaven," the subject of a number of his books.

Robert has been married to his high school sweetheart, Mary, for more than forty years. Blessed with six children and five grandchildren, they enjoy life together in beautiful Waco, Texas.